WATER
THE DROP OF LIFE

Companion to the

PUBLIC TELEVISION SERIES

BY PETER SWANSON

NORTHWORD PRESS
Minnetonka, Minnesota

Photography by SWYNK staff on location: Martin Struijf, Pieter Huisman, Louise Oeben, Paul King, Alexandra Jansse, Gilles Frenken, Upe van Leeuwen, Myra Konings, Stefano Bertacchini, Dennis Wielaert, Peter Swanson.

Johan Cruyff photo on pages 20 and 137 © Foto Leo Vogelenzang

Produced in association with 

SWYNK
Media Park, P. O. Box 2218
1200 CE Hilversum
Netherlands
www.swynk.nl

Executive Producers: John Wegink and Peter Gersen

Text by Bob Field, Katherine Deutch Tatlock, Peter Gersen, Peter Swanson
Edited by Barbara K. Harold
Designed by Russell S. Kuepper

NorthWord Press
5900 Green Oak Drive
Minnetonka, MN 55343
1-800-328-3895

ISBN 1-55971-782-3

Printed in U.S.A.

10 9 8 7 6 5 4 3 2 1

WATER

THE DROP OF LIFE

Companion to the

PUBLIC TELEVISION SERIES

BY PETER SWANSON

NorthWord Press
Minnetonka, Minnesota

TABLE OF CONTENTS

Foreword by Mikhail Gorbachev 7
Introduction 8

CHAPTER ONE	**Tampering with Mother Nature**	14
CHAPTER TWO	**The Spirit of Water**	24
CHAPTER THREE	**The Endless Search**	34
CHAPTER FOUR	**Our Daily Water**	46
CHAPTER FIVE	**A Price to Pay**	56
CHAPTER SIX	**The Aorta of Agriculture**	66
CHAPTER SEVEN	**The Way of the River**	76
CHAPTER EIGHT	**The Pipeline of Industry**	86
CHAPTER NINE	**The Perils of Pollution**	94
CHAPTER TEN	**The Challenge of Transportation**	104
CHAPTER ELEVEN	**Water—War and Peace**	116
CHAPTER TWELVE	**Facing the Future**	126

Biographies 138
Internet Sites 140
Film Credits 142
Index 143

FOREWORD

WATER, LIKE RELIGION and ideology, has the power to move millions of people. Since the very birth of human civilization, people have moved to settle close to it. People move when there is too little of it. People move when there is too much of it. People journey down it. People write, sing and dance about it. People fight over it. And all people, everywhere and every day, need it.

We need it for drinking, for cooking, for washing, for food, for sanitation, for industry, for energy, for transport, for rituals, for fun, for life. And it is not only we humans who need it; all life everywhere is dependent on water to survive.

But we stand today on the brink of a global water crisis. Although certain parts of the world have abundant water resources, supplies of drinking water are inadequate in many regions. Let us acknowledge that access to clean water is a universal human right, and in so doing accept that we have the corresponding universal responsibility to ensure that the forecast of a world where, in 25 years' time, two out of every three persons face water stress is proven wrong.

Without water security, social, economic and national stability are imperiled. This is magnified where water is shared across borders—and becomes crucial where water stress exists in regions of religious, territorial or ethnic tension. Thus we are faced with a mighty challenge.

Fortunately we have a history of meeting great challenges using imagination and our irrepressible capacity to adapt, and thousands of talented people around the world are already mobilized to the cause of preserving water for future generations.

Just as we are moved by water, we must now move in order to save it.

Mikhail Gorbachev
President, Green Cross International

INTRODUCTION

THIS IS THE STORY OF WATER.

IT IS A STORY OF LIFE . . . AND DEATH.

IT IS A STORY OF RICH . . . AND POOR.

IT IS A STORY OF BEAUTY . . . DESPAIR . . . CRISIS

. . . AND HOPE.

THE STORY OF WATER is told with the help of global personalities, people who believe that this may be the most important story of the new century.

In water, all of life's colors are reflected. In its timeless, nurturing grace, water inspires poets, artists, and world leaders alike.

World leaders such as U.N. Secretary-General Kofi Annan. *I'm someone who loves nature. One of the things I find most relaxing is to be in the woods, to be in the forest, to sit by the riverbank and watch the water flow by. I've got to this stage when I look at the river and I look at the water, what strikes me is how clean or dirty it is. But when you sit by a river that is clean, that has been protected, that has been respected by the inhabitants and you see the leaves flow by, it's so clean, you see the fish swimming, and all alone by the river, with birds singing, you realize how fortunate one is to be able to have that moment to be in nature and enjoy a river which is clean and alive.*

Water is constantly "alive." It is nature-in-motion—shape-changer, dazzler, master of deception. Water appears, disappears, and returns. As water changes, so does the course of humanity. One who has witnessed such changes is Shimon Peres, founder of the Peres Center for Peace. *Water streams through history as a very shining and challenging ingredient in the making of the people.*

Water is not only an ingredient in human history, it is the primary substance of the human body. Like Mother Earth, our bodies are 70 percent water. One could say that each of us—every man, woman, and child—is a small river, ebbing . . . flowing . . . seeking replenishment. A 1-percent deficiency of water in our body makes us thirsty, 5 percent causes a slight fever, and at 10 percent we become immobile. A 12-percent loss of water, and we die. There is no option, no alternative, no substitute. From the elderly to the young, the rivers within each one of us need a continuous supply of clean, fresh water.

The importance of water for a healthy body is crystal clear to World Cup soccer star and coach Johan Cruyff, now chairman of the Johan Cruyff Welfare Foundation. *Water is healthy, it's in our body and I drink a lot of water. You don't realize that it is so important because it is always there, it is just water. But it's the liquid that we live from, that we are from.*

Although our body's basic needs are the same for people all over the world, the amount of water we actually use in daily life differs enormously, depending on where we live or how much money we have. In Africa, an average Masai family survives on just over 1 gallon (4 liters) of water per person, per day. In Los Angeles, an average family uses almost 130 gallons (500 liters) of water per person, per day.

Our daily use of water is sometimes determined more by our attitudes than the geography of where we live. Attitudes about water are a concern of Tibet's spiritual leader, The Dalai Lama. *Without water we cannot survive. Water is the basis of our survival. Very important! Water also symbolizes the things which can purify.*

From far out in space, Earth looks like a great shining marble, its landmasses surrounded by dark blue liquid. From up there, it's hard to believe that we're approaching a world water crisis. The dominance of the color blue is very misleading. While water covers approximately 70 percent of Earth's surface, about 97 percent of it is saltwater. That leaves 3 percent freshwater, most of which is locked away in glaciers, icebergs, and snow.

What's left is found in either surface water—ponds, lakes, and rivers—or in aquifers—formations of groundwater—sunk deep below our feet. The sum total of all these available freshwater sources is a little less than 1 percent. Just 1 percent of Earth's water for all of humankind. With such a limited amount available it is cause for alarm that even our coastal waters are showing evidence of human toxic lifestyles.

Ted Danson, actor, environmentalist and President of the American Oceans Campaign, is working to stop the source of coastal pollution. *I am concerned about being able to swim and fish*

off the beaches. In that first thirty miles of coast, coastal waters. I'm concerned about that. Well, I cannot just look at that and say, What is the problem? I have to go to the top of the mountain. And I have to look at where the water comes from to begin with. And watch what happens as it goes all the way down. I mean, if you follow nature, you know the natural path of water, and you look at what we do to it, all the way down, that's where you have to solve the problem.

As water flows from the mountaintop to the sea, it carries evidence of humankind's collective irresponsibility. Every year, chemical contamination and waterborne diseases kill 15 million people. Some of this pollution comes from human waste, some from agricultural waste, and some from industrial waste. Together, they are choking our rivers and contaminating our groundwater. Painfully, we are learning that the penalty for polluting our water is severe. Every eight seconds . . . somewhere in the world . . . a child dies of a water-related disease.

For many years, prize-winning author and environmentalist Isabel Allende has been concerned about these disturbing developments. *Water symbolizes everything that is fresh and renewed and transformed in us as human beings. Clean, running water is an incredibly precious thing that not everybody has, very few people have. Even in the United States, for example, you go to a hotel and it is indicated that you cannot drink the water; you have to use bottled water.*

Awareness of water often depends on how accessible the water is. Surprisingly, in today's high-tech world, one out of every six people must still hand-carry this heavy liquid, often over long distances, from the source to their home.

Mikhail Gorbachev, now President of Green Cross International, has a global perspective on the distribution of water. *There are problems concerning utilization of the river Jordan, water problems in the northeast of Latin America, problems between India and Bangladesh. All these problems are caused by shortage of water. Water problems concern a number of countries concentrated in the areas around the rivers and in the basins of certain rivers. It is really important to solve the problem of rational utilization and distribution of water supplies. I dare say, the shortage of freshwater is the major ecological problem of this moment.*

Whether by foot or by machine, the need to transport water is universal. Water transportation systems come in many forms. The construction and maintenance of these systems always involves money.

For the poor this financial burden is especially high, and some pay as much as 20 percent of their income to private water vendors. As water comes to us through a pipeline, from a truck, or via subsidized tap, there is a price to pay. Who owns the resource and controls the price is a concern for business leader Anita Roddick, founder of The Body Shop. *One of the great tragedies is when the resource has an economic value for a few people, rather than for the community that should share it. I think that's a huge dilemma.*

The price of water is of special concern to farmers because they use more of it than anyone else. Agriculture uses no less than 70 percent of our freshwater supply. Our daily food depends on water. With huge agri-businesses trying to keep up with a growing demand for food, farmers are beginning to see limits of production capacity.

The heritage of Jimmy Carter, former President of the United States, springs from the soil. He sees the agricultural issues very clearly. *As a farmer myself I still see the problem of water, but it has changed dramatically since I was a boy. Back then, there was no such thing as irrigation. All of the natural erupting springs out of the ground were flowing and the streams were full of water. And then along came irrigation, where tremendous wells were dug and vast quantities of water were spread into the air, some of which falls on the crops and makes them grow. And now, the water level, the subterranean water level, the aquifer, is falling very rapidly. And the farmers know it. And now it's very difficult to get a permit to dig another irrigation well. So I think for the first time in history, Georgia farmers, the ones I know, are beginning to realize that they have to conserve water.*

Conservation is one of the keys to the future of water because nations are running low on clean water. Water for drinking, cooking, and cleansing. Water for power, industry, shaping our destiny.

Nations today value water as the key to their continued development. As competition for quality water that flows across international boundaries increases, some nations are prepared to fight to ensure their share of water.

One whose life and country is influenced by that tension is Jordan's Queen Noor. *As a citizen of the Middle East, I am acutely conscious of the potential [water] has for conflict as well as [being] a finite resource, and one that we in our region recognize, that we suffer more acute water shortage than any other region in the world and have seen and continue to live with the pressure of conflict and competition over this precious resource. It is something we can't take for granted and a very important part of every aspect of our lives.*

Smoke and rubble of future water wars. Noxious filth in polluted rivers. Fields turned to salt from poor drainage. The people of the world are facing their biggest challenge ever. A challenge that will be passed on to generations to come. The challenge of water.

By the year 2020, nearly fifty nations will suffer severe water shortages. By 2025, more than a dozen nations will need water from rivers controlled by hostile neighbors. By 2030, many cities that have existed for centuries will simply dry up. Six billion people now inhabit Earth. By the year 2050, that figure may double. Yet, the planet's available water supply will remain the same. And the quality of this supply is deteriorating.

Ted Danson sums it up. *I guess it is good news/bad news, you know. The bad news is that we are running out of water, we are overusing it, using it poorly, polluting it, poisoning it. But the good news is that we are going to have to do something about it. The reason we need a plan is we are having problems now with the population on the earth being many billions. In 50, 60 years they say we will double our population. Boy, you better have a plan. You better start reusing and conserving your water, because it will become the issue.*

Indeed, a plan for water is long overdue. A plan that involves every key player in our global society, from industries to politicians. However, real change begins with people. History has proven that individuals do make a difference.

Kofi Annan expressed it this way. *What I would say is that individuals should never underestimate their own influence and the role they can play in changing things for the better. I think they should speak up in their communities and say: "Stop polluting our rivers. Stop wasting water. I can't take this anymore." And begin to talk to their neighbors and friends, and begin to organize and let the policy makers and the local, district, or national governments know that they are concerned. There is a lot of material on this out there and they can organize themselves, share the information with their friends, and challenge their governments.*

This book and its companion public television series hope to inspire individuals. Through inspiration we hope to help build an awareness of the need to preserve and protect the precious resource that flows through each and every one of us—*Water: The Drop of Life.* ■

For hundreds of different mammals or insects or flies, all have the common, I think, same sort of sense. You see, they love water.

The Dalai Lama

The Middle East is becoming slowly a desert.

Shimon Peres

One really important thing is to be re-enchanted by water. I think your experiences change, your values change, your thoughts about water will change when your experiences with it change.

Anita Roddick

CHAPTER ONE

Tampering with Mother Nature

HABITATS ARE DEFINED as environments that are the homes of living creatures. All over the world, Mother Nature provides a variety of habitats, unique places, that support a diversity of life. Some, like our oceans, are liquid. Some, like our vast deserts, are parched from blistering heat. Others are vistas of frozen wilderness. Still others endure great ranges of temperature and humidity as the earth circles the sun. Somehow life has found a way to thrive in these varied environments. Different creatures. Different plants. Different needs. But regardless of their differences, each living thing is dependent on one precious resource, water.

In both water-scarce and water-abundant regions, the balance between Mother Nature's gifts and the way they are used is often critical. Adaptability is what sustains life and maintains balance for plant and animal species, regardless of where they live.

Human beings also live in these diverse environs. Rather than adapting to the habitat, too often humans try to alter the environment to meet their needs. In doing so, we upset Mother Nature's balance. We somehow feel that we are apart from nature and not liable to her laws. However, at the dawn of the new millennium, we are discovering that Mother Nature's laws are supreme. We do, in fact, depend on her delicate harmony, especially when it comes to the need for water.

■ ■ ■ The Namib Desert—DISTURBING THE BALANCE

DESERTS ARE PLACES of searing heat and shifting sands; habitats accustomed to scarcity. Yet even here, in these bone-dry conditions, life adapts.

The Namib in Africa is one of the world's driest deserts. Some years, no rain at all falls on this place. But a huge variety of life forms adapt to the desert's harsh environment.

For example, along the coastal strip of the Namib, "fog" rises off the Atlantic Ocean and drifts across the land. Here, the *Welwitschia mirabilis* plant thrives on moisture derived from this fog, despite growing in an area 25 to 75 miles (40 to 120 kilometers) away from the coast. And the aptly named fog beetle collects drops of water on its back to survive in the mountains of sand.

In the Outer Namib, the rattlesnake's distinctive navigation technique and its habit of burrowing deep into the desert sand keep its body temperature stable. Like the plants and insects that share its harsh habitat, this clever reptile has learned to adapt.

But unlike other animals, human adaptation to the desert environment has not always been in balance with the surroundings. For instance, the introduction of domesticated animals is upsetting the natural balance. Farmers have brought goats to the Namib. Goats often rip out indigenous grasses and plants, vegetation that stores precious liquid in a water-stressed terrain. This depletion is causing the Namib Desert to spread.

Ultimately, the human being is in the mercy of nature.

The Dalai Lama

It is not only that goats overgraze; the problem of imbalance is often compounded by the goat-herders themselves. Namib herdsmen and villagers routinely collect firewood. But tree roots hold down the sand, preventing the desert from spreading further. Fewer roots, more sand.

To many of us, goat grazing and wood gathering may seem like small intrusions. But without proper understanding, even the smallest intrusion can tip the scales and upset the balance of nature's systems. ■

There is a lot that came before me. And, hopefully there will be a lot that comes after me. And it's not about you, it's not about your time here. It's about your stewardship of what you inherit and how well you take care of it and pass it on.

Ted Danson

Interesting Facts . . .

- The Namib is thought to be the oldest arid region in the world.
- In the Nama language, Namib means "vast."
- The Namib Desert is about 1,240 miles (2,000 kilometers) long, hugging the southwestern coast of Africa from Angola to South Africa.
- The *Welwitschia mirabilis* plant has only two leaves and may live for 2,000 years.

■ ■ ■ Glen Canyon Dam—ALTERING THE FLOW

FOR THOUSANDS OF YEARS, the great Colorado River thundered freely through Glen Canyon. This is an area where human intrusion on a grand scale has been the source of a forty-year-long debate. Since its completion in 1963, the Glen Canyon Dam has been diverting water from the Colorado to farms, ranches, cities, and towns in several states. Turbines from the great dam provide electricity to areas of California, Arizona, and Utah.

But Glen Canyon Dam is blocking Mother Nature's flow. In southern Utah, the great dam has altered the timeless flow of the Colorado River. It has eliminated the natural cycle of annual spring floods. These annual floods had the positive effect of forming sandbars along the river. Now, virtually all sediment is trapped above the great dam in Lake Powell. Without any sediment being deposited downstream, sandbars have been eroding and steadily disappearing. This, in turn, is reducing the backwater habitat available for numerous species.

A backwater is like a nursery for young fish. It is a habitat that forms in association with sandbars. It's an environment that warms substantially above the river temperature to provide a good warm-water habitat in which young fish grow and prosper.

As ecological problems have increased, Glen Canyon Dam authorities have opted to borrow from one of Mother Nature's designs. In March 1996, they experimented with a controlled high-flow release by shooting huge amounts of water through four giant steel tubes at the base of the dam.

The artificial flood was designed to reproduce the dynamics of a natural river flow. Records show that the 1996 controlled release helped the Colorado River downstream to rise 16 feet (5 meters) higher than usual—beaches increased by 30 percent.

And engineers point to new evidence indicating another positive result from the controlled release. Native fish are already returning to the river habitat, fish like the nearly extinct humpback chub. Peregrine falcons, which are an endangered raptor, also live and hunt in this section of Glen Canyon. They feed on the fowl in the river system. This is just one small example that teaches a simple truth: In all nature's systems you cannot disturb one part without having a profound effect on other parts.

While the controlled floods have had some success, the Colorado River has not been fully restored. Many of the new sandbars have eroded away. Some believe that the dam should be removed, letting the river run freely once again. The controversy, unlike the river, rages on. ■

Nature has this way to filter and clean and rejuvenate itself. But when we come in and conquer nature and go: you know, we are going to put concrete right here, and we are going to put a dam here. Well, that has a huge impact.

Ted Danson

Interesting Facts . . .

- It is estimated that Lake Powell loses about 2 percent of its water each year to evaporation.
- The Glen Canyon Dam's eight generating units provide a total generating capacity of 1,296,000 kilowatts.
- Structural height: 710 feet (216.4 meters)
- Base width: 300 feet (91.4 meters)
- Crest width: 25 feet (7.6 meters)
- Crest length: 1,560 feet (475.5 meters)
- Volume of concrete: 4,901,000 cubic yards (3,724,760 cubic meters)

■ ■ ■ The Biesbosch—A WETLAND IN TROUBLE

AS WE SEEK TO FIND a balance in our growth and development, we need to understand that some environments are crucial to the development of all life. Wetlands are the nurseries of Mother Nature. Currently, 2 percent of the earth's total surface is wetland, formed by fresh water, salt water, or a combination of both. Coastal wetlands are areas where fresh water and salt water meet. These environments are critical breeding grounds on which a multitude of species depends.

When it rains heavily, wetlands act like giant sponges soaking up excess water as it spreads. Wetlands act as natural filters, cleaning the water that passes through them. Yet for all their benefits, the earth's wetlands are among the most endangered of all habitats, because of human intervention.

Translated to mean "reed forest," the Biesbosch is one of the few remaining wetland parks in the Netherlands. Every spring great flocks of birds nest safely in this labyrinth of inlets, marshes, and tidal creeks. They feed on the diversity of organisms nourished by the tides.

The Netherlands was originally a grand wetland, dominated by the rivers Rhine and Maas. Since the thirteenth century, Dutch farmers have drained wetlands to create small farms, or polders. Dikes and canals were built to divert water around land needed for a growing population. The great rivers were channeled to create more land and a better infrastructure for commercial shipping. Wetland areas decreased in size and number.

In 1953, disaster struck. Storms from the North Sea caused floods that inundated much of the southwestern coast, killing over 1,800 people. The Dutch government decided to build an extensive system of dikes and dams known as the Delta Works. This project was designed to keep the country from ever flooding again.

But as so often happens when humans intervene in Mother Nature's plan, unexpected consequences arose. The great seawall stopped the flushing actions of the tides, leaving marsh areas like the Biesbosch stagnant. Rare plants became overgrown with common botanical varieties, and the reeds and willows were mostly lost.

I don't think that a lot of people would think that Holland would have a problem with water. Everybody would say, "Now that's ridiculous." But it is like that, there is a serious problem, even for a country like Holland.

Johan Cruyff

This massive intervention has still not secured the country from floods. Over the years, the channeling of the rivers and the reclaiming of land for farms and growing cities have destroyed the natural flood control mechanisms. Wetland parks like the Biesbosch are simply too small to handle any excess water from the rivers Maas and Waal. The country is now in danger of flooding from the rivers rather than the sea.

The government is now rethinking its development policy. A program has been proposed to buy back polders and let them grow wild. This will help absorb overflow, and the rivers will have more room again. Wild species of cattle that graze in irregular patterns have been introduced in these areas to help create more diverse landscapes. Diverse landscapes will promote greater variety in animals and plants, which will aid in restoring a healthy wetland habitat.

And the giant doors on the great seawalls are being opened to allow tidal flushing once again. The people of this country are engaged in an effort to reclaim nature's gifts that were nearly lost forever. ■

We have to take care about nature as much as nature is taking care about us. Nature is very kind with us. And if you want to enjoy the gifts of nature and the promises of nature, we have to defer to nature and its needs, its rules, its norms.

Shimon Peres

Interesting Facts . . .

- Wetlands are found from the tundra to the tropics and on every continent except Antarctica.
- Even when wetlands appear dry, they still provide critical habitat for many creatures. One acre (0.4 hectare) of wetlands stores up to 1.5 million gallons (5.68 million liters) of flood water.
- In 1983, the U.S. Army Corps of Engineers reported that the wetlands along the Charles River near Boston were responsible for saving $17 million (£11.8 million) in flood damage each year.

We have wasted a great deal of the donations of nature—we cut the trees, we polluted the rivers, we polluted the air. And we must understand that we are now beginning to pay the price for it.

Shimon Peres

Guardians of the Rainforest

IN ECUADOR, the price of losing the rainforest to developmental pressures could be extreme. The Amazon is a haunting, complex environment teeming with life. Along its total length, the Amazon Basin touches nine different nations. This rainforest habitat holds over one-fifth of the world's fresh water.

With extraordinary bio-diversity, rainforests are one of the great collective treasures of Mother Nature. The Amazon River Basin is home to more than one-third of all species of animals. Fortunately, at least one group of humans has learned to survive in this environment.

They call themselves "Guardians of the Rainforest." They are the Cofan, the indigenous people of the Ecuadorian Amazon region. Water has always been the center of their lives. For years, many Cofan have lived along the Dureno River, a tributary of the Amazon. The Cofan learned early of Mother Nature's bountiful gifts. The rainforest is their pharmacy. They use plants such as shendu to help with burning pains, and husindi to cure earaches.

The rainforest is also our pharmacy. About one-fourth of all the medicines we use today come from rainforest plants. In fact, more than 1,400 varieties of tropical plants are thought to be potential cures for cancer.

In this habitat, the Cofan have lived in harmony with nature, cut off from the outside world for centuries. But starting in 1971, that harmony was abruptly disturbed. A U.S. petroleum company working in consort with the state oil company of Ecuador started drilling for oil in the Cuyabeno Reserve. Wastewater from the oil company's operations was routinely dumped into the Dureno River. Pipeline accidents were frequent and oil slicks added further contamination to the river.

In 1992, the U.S. company ceased its operations in the Cuyabeno Reserve. But the Ecuadorian company continued the environmental nightmare. Today, hundreds of waste pits are still being used, and toxic wastewater is still being dumped at an alarming rate. Fiery toxic fumes are creating an acid rainfall. The wanton contamination of this delicate ecosystem has wreaked havoc on the world of the Cofan.

Romelia Mendoa, a Cofan woman, talks about the changes to her world: "The entire river is dirty now. Because the river has become so filthy, we can no longer bathe in it. All sorts of sickness have come to us from the pollution that can now be found in the river. We can't do anything with it, not even wash our clothes. If we swim in it, we get skin problems with our bodies. It is impossible to use the water to drink or prepare drinks with it. We have had to make wells to drink from. Also, look at my feet, how they have become diseased. We are suffering a lot from sicknesses like this. We also suffer from other oil-related illnesses. As I was saying earlier, if we had not dug wells and continued to drink the water, we would have died of drinking kerosene-polluted water."

In the case of the Cofan, changes made by oil pollution have forced them to move to an area known as Zabalo. But will Zabalo remain pure and clean for long? As civilization encroaches on the wilderness, an estimated 49 million acres (20 million hectares) of rainforest land are wiped out each year.

Perhaps it is time for a new way of thinking as we seek to live and grow in balance with nature's habitats. We must find new ways of developing our communities before the balance can be restored; before a sustainable future can be assured for all life on Earth. ■

Water is considered the source of survival. Maybe we can describe it as one truth.
The Dalai Lama

Interesting Facts . . .

- While the Ecuadorian rainforest is only about 2 percent of the land area of the Amazon Basin, it contains about one-third of its total bio-diversity. One of the reasons for this amazing diversity is that the region escaped the last ice age.
- The Cuyabeno Reserve preserves over 1.5 million acres (603,000 hectares) of land in northeast Ecuador.
- In just 2.5 acres (1 hectare) of the Cuyabeno Reserve, 473 different species of trees can be found. The reserve contains over 500 species of birds, 250 species of fish, and 100 species of mammals.
- In twenty years of oil production, over 2.5 million acres (1 million hectares) of rain forest have been lost in the construction of roads and oil-related facilities.

I go back to the Holy Koran,
water is the source of life,
a source of renewal of life and
hope in this region.

Queen Noor of Jordan

The whole spiritual thing is... really about people feeling like they matter. That they care. That they can make a difference. If you teach little kids that they make a difference in the world, that they matter, that they are special, you will create a climate where people take care of things. Where they take care of nature. Where they realize that they are part of nature. That they are part of the life cycle. And we sometimes forget that.

Ted Danson

CHAPTER TWO

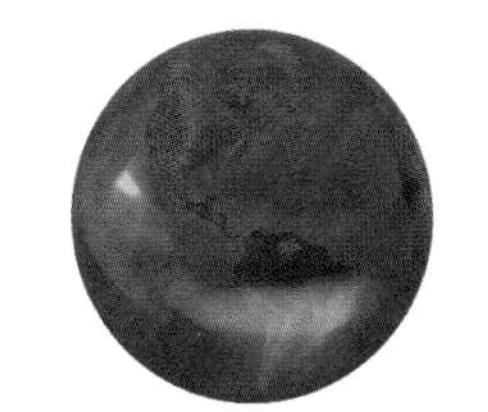

The Spirit of Water

WHAT IS THE SPIRIT OF WATER? Just as a river carries minerals and sediment downstream, water also carries many meanings wherever it flows. Since ancient times water has been cherished and even worshipped as a source of life. Water has also been feared as a great destructive force through violent storms and raging floods. Water cycles have been forever tied to life and death.

The cleansing power of water is recognized in most spiritual traditions. In the Moslem faith, for example, the ritual washing of hands and feet before entering the temple is an act of purification. But water is also capable of harboring bacteria, disease, and plague.

Creation, destruction, purification, and pollution. With such powerful properties, it is no wonder that humans have integrated water into ritual life. In ritual, we often seek to commune with that which is holy, that which has power. If rituals teach us anything, it is the obvious but easily ignored respect for water.

▪ ▪ ▪ Japanese Tea Ceremony—A WAY OF LIFE

IN THE FRENZY of a business day in a large Japanese city, rituals may at first seem long forgotten. Yet this is an illusion. In modern Japan, time-honored rituals of water are ever present. In fact, items of everyday life, such as a cup of tea, are often honored in these rituals.

The Japanese Tea Ceremony is a water ritual that encompasses the four principles essential to a state of grace: Purity, Respect, Tranquility, and Harmony. The washing and rinsing of each bowl, each utensil, before making the tea, symbolizes Purity, the purity of daily water that must be preserved.

Carefully, respectfully, the tea master places the tea in the bowl. Like humans and nature, Respect binds the host and guest together in The Way of Tea. Regardless of outside pressures, there is always time for Respect.

Silently, water is added to the tea. Tranquility is a natural aesthetic of water, the grace and beauty of life observed and maintained.

With tranquil reverence the tea is passed to each guest at the ceremony, bringing the group into Harmony. Harmony allows for space between things. The Tea Ceremony observes mankind in harmony with nature's rhythms.

In ritual, as in earthly balance, nature and mankind give and receive in an atmosphere of reverence. Life is restored; the future is sustained. ■

Ancient cultures and cities have always sprung up on the banks of the river, going back to Mesopotamia.
Kofi Annan

Interesting Facts . . .

- Tea was originally a medicine that was brought from southern Asia to China.
- The tea used in the Tea Ceremony is Matcha, a bitter green tea ground into a fine powder.
- Sen Rikyu (1522-1591) is the tea master who is credited with creating the Tea Ceremony. He turned a simple daily event into a philosophy for a way of life, The Way of Tea.
- In many countries it is possible to take lessons in The Way of Tea.

■ ■ ■ Blessing of the Harvest in Bali—AN AMAZING GRACE

IN RITUAL, the daily reality of everyday life, such as the growing of food for our survival, is connected with the realm of the spirit.

In a temple built atop a natural spring in Bali, Indonesia, the steady gaze and measured hand of a high priest prepares the offering. It is water—pure, treasured, and holy. Flowers, oils, and spices are added by this highest of Brahman priests as the water is readied for the blessing of the harvest.

People from the community bring elaborate baskets of fruit and vegetables as offerings to the temple deities. The offerings are blessed with the holy water, as are the people. Grains of rice are offered to them as symbols of the crop that sustains this community. The recipients—men, women, and children—place a grain of rice on their forehead. A consciousness is passed from generation to generation; the cycle continues. Carefully, gracefully, a tradition is preserved.

The baskets blessed with holy water are returned to the fields. For it is water that blesses the community. Water that envelops the young shoots that mature in this island's rice paddies. Water that will safeguard the coming harvest. ■

If you want to symbolize life, it's a bowl of water. It has to do with everything that is spiritual to humankind. In all harvest rituals water is involved, because there would be no harvesting without the water.

Isabel Allende

Interesting Facts . . .

- A Brahman is a Hindu priest who is a spiritual advisor to families and communities, and is always consulted for ceremonies when holy water is called for.
- The Hindus of Bali believe that Lord Vishnu caused the earth to give birth to rice.
- The goddess of rice is Dewi Sri, who is both male and female. In Bali, rice fields are adorned with fruit offerings to this goddess.
- Grains of rice are often prepared with banana leaves and left on the ground to keep the evil spirits away.
- Harvest rituals vary in size and scope from a simple grace to elaborate ceremonies.

■ ■ ■ Initiation of a Shinto Priest—CONTACT WITH THE GODS

A SPIRITUAL CONNECTION with elements like water is a primary force in the life of a Shinto priest. Within the Tsuruqaoka Hachimanqu Shrine, an eleventh-century ceremony of purification is preserved by Shinto initiates of modern Japan. After deeply bowing to the deities, and dressed only in a fundoshi—a loincloth—the guji, or high priest, claps his hands twice and begins a ritual shaking of his hands and chanting an invocation to the gods.

The gods of Shinto are nature gods called "kami." The kami may be anything that is extraordinary and that inspires awe or reverence. Water is one of the most revered of kami. Immersing oneself in water is considered by many to be the most intimate contact one might have with a deity.

An assembled group of priests-to-be, also in loincloths, are being led by the guji in a chant in which they ask the deities to cleanse their souls and bodies so they can be worthy of the priesthood. Standing with one foot in front of the other, they begin a rowing motion and a new, vigorous chant. They are preparing their bodies for contact with the kami.

After the chanting, they immerse themselves in water and continue to pray. Purification is central to the Shinto religion and water is the key to purification. Often, purification is done near a river in the belief that the river will wash away all impurities. Immersed in water these initiates seek cosmic harmony, to be in unity with nature.

In the words of Shihego Yoshida, the Shinto priest leading the ceremony: "Shintoism was created by the old Japanese, a people of farmers. They respected the forces of nature and lived with great honor for these forces of nature. They saw spirits in everything around them.

So, there's a reverence, which we don't have in our society. We have a respect, you know, we clean up our mess, or we should. We have a respect about how water comes and how we should preserve it. But that spiritual relationship with the world, with the plant world, or with the ground, or with water, we don't have. And that's a lesson—a huge lesson—for us I think, in the West. To be able to take these rituals and get a sense of reverence which we don't have now.

Anita Roddick

Furthermore they believed that water contained special qualities. First of all it cleanses and purifies of dirt, of impurity. In and outside the body, water brings new forces. People still believe this. This is one of the basic assumptions of Shintoism."

Co-existence with the natural world, with the spirits of the world, with the cycles of Mother Nature—especially those of water—all are observed in the respectful and practical rituals of Shinto. ■

It's those types of rituals that I think are the sort of myths and legends of life that we've lost in our society. We don't know how to ritualize water. We just turn on the tap and there it comes, but we don't have the sense of benediction for water.

Anita Roddick

Interesting Facts . . .

- The word Shinto means "the Way of the Gods," and comes from two Chinese words: *Shin*, meaning "divinity," and *Tao,* meaning "the way."
- Shinto is an ancient religion dating back to at least 500 BC with no holy texts and no original founder. After World War II, the Shinto priesthood was open to women.
- There are over 110,000 Shinto shrines and temples for the kami in Japan. The gate of a Shinto shrine is called a *tori*, and marks the boundary between the finite and the infinite.
- The art of origami comes from the Shintoism, and many Shinto shrines are decorated with this "paper of the spirits."

■ ■ ■ Baptism in the Jordan River—DOWN BY THE RIVERSIDE

ANOTHER RITUAL that involves immersion in water is baptism, a rite of purification by water. Although the ritual of baptism is observed in houses of worship and along riverbanks all over the world, the site on the Jordan River at Yardenit, near where the Jordan River flows south from of the Sea of Galilee in Israel, continues to be the most holy of all baptism sites. Christian tradition states that it was here, in the time of Roman conquerors, that Christ chose to be anointed with the "waters-of-forgiveness" by John the Baptist.

For Christians, baptism is a sacrament, a visible and symbolic action with inward and spiritual meaning. The visible action is immersion in water. Christians believe their sins are immersed and forgiven in the death of Christ, that with Christ's resurrection they are reborn into a new life. In water their bodies and spirits are cleansed anew.

In baptism, water is a symbol of both death and new life. There is recognition that water has destructive powers, such as in the great flood of Noah's time. But there is also a primal creative power of water that is poetically phrased in Genesis: "Now the earth was formless and empty, darkness was over the surface of the deep, and the Spirit of God was hovering over the waters. And God said, 'Let there be light,' and there was light."

Baptism as a ritual is practiced in the spirit of Christ's directive to his disciples in Matthew: "And Jesus came and spoke to them, saying, 'All power has been given to me in heaven and on earth. Go, therefore, and make disciples of all nations, baptizing them in the name of the Father, and of the Son, and of the Holy Spirit.'"

Like the waters that flow through the Jordan River, Christians believe that Christ's spirit flows though the bodies of his followers. ■

Water has been present in most spiritual rituals all over the world in many ways. Of course, here in the western world, we relate to baptism, for example. In the Catholic Church you sprinkle water on the child. In other churches, Christian churches, you have to go completely into the water, in a river or in a lake. The idea is that you have to purify; water is something that cleanses you inside out.

Isabel Allende

The Jordan River throughout history and throughout the spiritual history of our region as well as economic, political, and social [history] has been a symbol as well as a wellspring of spirit and life and health. And a very clear blessing of God.

Queen Noor of Jordan

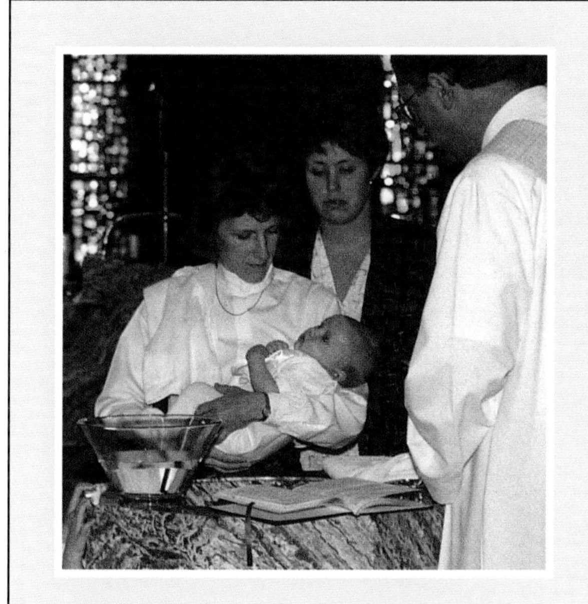

Interesting Facts . . .

- The word baptism is from the Greek word *baptizo*, meaning "to immerse."
- The Christian practice of immersion in water descended from the Jewish practice, outlined in the book of Leviticus.
- Archaeologists are excavating an ancient village thought to be the home of John the Baptist near Bethany in Israel.
- The practice of infant baptism did not become a normal practice until the fifth century, and there is still a debate today as to whether or not this constitutes a proper baptism.

▪ ▪ ▪ Cremation at Varanasi—THE MOST HOLY DEATH

VARANASI, INDIA, has been called the holiest of holies, the "last city" of the Hindus.

Here, carpet weavers, boatmen, and beggars join in daily observance of a cosmic ritual along the banks of the sacred Ganges River. Also known as "the City of Death," Varanasi is a place where millions from all over India come for the ritual of endings, and of beginnings—the ritual of cremation.

Bodies are often carried for hours through the streets of this eternal city before they arrive at the banks of the Mother River. An initial immersion of the person in the holy river cleanses the body of all sins and prepares it for cremation. Cremation is more than disposing of a body; it is an act of renewal, for fire is not just a consumer of flesh, but a producer of heat, a creator of life.

Manikarnika Ghat is Varanasi's main crematorium and the place where, according to legend, the world was created at the beginning of time, and where the corpse of the cosmos will be burned at the end of time. Here the wood is stacked in pyres, for the fire that will totally consume loved ones.

A cremation at Varanasi is an attempt to break the earthly cycles. It is said that if you die in Varanasi your spirit will transcend the cycle of death and rebirth and go directly to Moksha. You will achieve Nirvana.

Symbolizing the destruction of our earthly bodies, a clay pot filled with holy Ganges water is thrust upon the fire. A member of the family, most always a male with his head shaven for the occasion, stands facing away from the fire. Holding the pot in front of him he thrusts it over his head and backward onto the funeral pyre. He then performs the most solemn of tasks. The charred earthly remains of the body are returned to the Ganges, holiest of rivers.

According to Hindu legend, the Ganges is the one river that flows beyond its earthly bounds carrying all that is within to the realm of Moksha.

In Varanasi, the rituals go on—rituals that teach us that our living and our dying are forever interwoven with the cycles of water. ■

You look at the Ganges in India and it shows you that instinctively, not only do we value the importance of water, but we want to be close to it, we want to have access to it. So all these big cities, and civilizations, developed along water, and people really see water as a source of life.

Kofi Annan

Interesting Facts . . .

- In Varanasi, over 60,000 people bathe in the Ganges River every day.
- The city of Varanasi is over 3,000 years old and is also known by the names Banaras and Kashi. It is a holy city and is said to be the dwelling place of the god Shiva.
- The river Ganges begins in the glaciers of the Himalayas and flows about 1,557 miles (2,506 kilometers) eastward to the Bay of Bengal.
- The paradox of the Ganges is that it is revered as a holy symbol of life by hundreds of millions of Hindus, yet it is terribly polluted.

It is an issue of the sustainability of our futures, all of us, as we are intertwined.

Queen Noor of Jordan

You cannot be a dry person and you shouldn't be a dry country.

Shimon Peres

Overpopulation, overexploitation of the resources, abuse of the environment is creating an intolerable way of living.

Isabel Allende

CHAPTER THREE

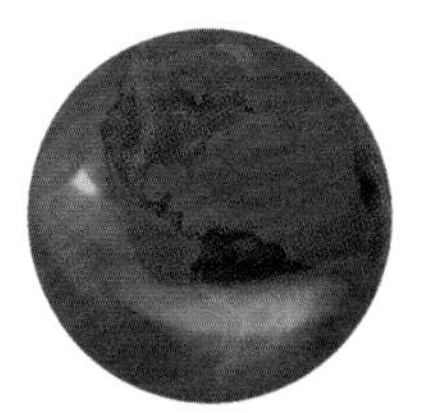

The Endless Search

LIVING BY THE WATER'S EDGE sustained early communities of humans. But the river was not always dependable. Seasons of drought sometimes dried up the life-giving waters. Through hard lessons of famine, people learned to conserve and collect water to nourish themselves in dry times.

Drought, flood, population growth, and simple curiosity also motivated people to move. With movement came the need to find new water, for its sheer weight made it impractical to carry over long distances. In the search for new sources of water, people looked to nature's clues. By following animals, understanding terrain, and sensing the winds, early humans had great success in their quest for water.

Indigenous peoples have always retained an intimate knowledge of their surroundings. Somewhere along the line of history, the so-called "developed world" has lost this keen connection to the environment. In looking at the ways native peoples searched for, collected, and cared for water, we may be helped in our modern-day quest for sustainable supplies of this precious liquid.

The future of the people of the world depends on this search. While many take it for granted, millions struggle every day in their ever-more-urgent search for water.

■ ■ ■ The Kalahari Bushmen—A HUNT FOR HIDDEN WATER

THE SCENE IS southern Africa. Across a wind-blown landscape, Mother Nature leaves clues for two searchers. On this quest, hunters from the disappearing San tribe of Kalahari Bushmen track a small herd of gemsbok. Not for food, but for water.

The San are keen hunters. They are intimately aware of their environment and they know that the gemsbok will lead them to the sweet-tasting tsama. It is a melon that, with its liquid, sustains both humans and animals in a land that lacks permanent water.

Usually people were concentrated around wells and rivers; some of the dry rivers were apparently richer in water than they are today, but people of our region suffered throughout history for the lack of water.

Shimon Peres

During the dry summer months, there are many days when the San consume nothing but tsama—no other food, no water, only tsama.

Today, the hunters are successful, and members of the tribe celebrate their bounty. A tribal shaman, called Ma, builds a sacred altar around a small tree limb in praise of their find. She includes a gunu plant, a source of strong magic. Ma then performs a ritual dance dating back to the Stone Age. She implores the gods to bring rain to the parched land and provide the San temporary relief in their endless search for water. ■

We need a global approach to this from all sides. We need to educate people, we need the scientists to create new technologies, we need the engineers to create the networks, we need every human being to be aware of how precious water is and save it. Don't waste it. Everybody has to be involved in a very firm and assertive way.

Isabel Allende

Interesting Facts . . .

- Temperatures in the Kalahari Desert can reach 120 degrees Fahrenheit (49 degrees Celsius). It receives between 4 and 30 inches (100 and 750 millimeters) of rain each year between April and November.
- The word *San* means "food gatherers." The San are members of a people who have roamed Africa for over 30,000 years.
- The name Kalahari comes from the word *Kgalagadi,* which is a Tswana word meaning "the great thirst."

Petra—A STUDY OF ANCIENT ENGINEERING

AS THE STORY goes, seeking divine help in the quest for water has sometimes yielded tangible results. According to tradition, Moses hit a stone with a stick and extracted water from it. That was the first miracle.

After thousands of years, the miracle of Ain Musa, "the Well of Moses," is still a place where Jordanians find water.

Those who do not settle near water must use their ingenuity to find and transport it. Such is the case in Petra, known as the mystic city. Hidden among age-old canyons, it is a shining monument to the industrious Nabataeans, an Arab people who settled in southern Jordan 2,000 years ago.

Like many ancient peoples, the first place the Nabataeans looked in their search for water was to the sky. But although the gods answered with 6 precious inches (152 millimeters) of rain per year, 92 percent of it was lost to evaporation. To compensate for this loss, each family had at least one cistern for collecting rainwater. Some were sophisticated systems, with sedimentation basins to separate mud and sand before the water entered the containment portion of the cistern so the water would be fit for drinking.

But since rainwater was not adequate for the Nabataeans' survival, and there were no springs to be found in the great canyon walls, they had to use their ingenuity to transport water from distant wells such as Ain Musa.

These ancient engineers used a network of wadis, channels, and terraces, plus dams, pipes, and cisterns to collect, store, and deliver water to a civilization of 30,000 people. Canals were dug out of the limestone canyon walls and gravity was used to transport the water.

Modern engineers have begun to retrace and map the Nabataean system. They have discovered some principles that can be applied to today's needs. For example, the ancient ceramic water pipes recently discovered in the Sig, one of Petra's narrow canyons, demonstrate an understanding that drinking water had to be transported in a special way. The canals meant for drinking water were lined with a special coating to keep the water clean.

Balancing development and the environment is a problem we all face. Lessons from ancient peoples often endure in places that suffer from lack of water. ■

In Petra we see today actually the artifacts, the remains, of [the Nabataeans'] extremely professional, scientific, and successful water management system. It's an extremely impressive system that is visible today, and is one example of the ways in which they were very conscious of the need to balance environmental conservation needs against human development needs.

Queen Noor of Jordan

Interesting Facts . . .

- In Greek, *Petra* means "Rock."
- One 54-cubic-yard (40-cubic-meter) cistern could hold enough water to sustain a family for months. This enabled the citizens of Petra to outlast invading armies.
- The water canals of Petra contained an elaborate system of levels to filter water, and gates to divert it to where it was needed.

Cattle Ranching in the Australian Outback—LESSONS FROM THE ABORIGINES

THOUSANDS OF MILES from the land of Moses lies the Australian Outback—a barren, hot, and dry region that challenges all life forms. With the average cow consuming 15 gallons (57 liters) of water per day, cattle ranching would seem an unlikely endeavor in this drought-prone area. Yet Donald Holt comes from a long line of cattle ranchers who continue to prosper near the desolate town of Alice Springs.

He says there are advantages to raising beef in this region. "We have a shortage of rain, but we have other advantages. There is no disease here—none whatsoever. No worms, no lice, no ticks, no mad cow disease. The cattle are very healthy. So it's a big advantage."

To meet the water needs of thousands of thirsty cows, the Holt family realized that it had to first seek an understanding of their environment. Recalling his family history, Donald pays respect to the native people of this dry land. "When my ancestors first came here, they were totally relying on the aboriginal people to guide them to water.

"Over several generations, we've learned a lot from the aboriginal peoples, particularly about how to observe what's happening around you, where the water runs, when the rains come, and what to do when it doesn't come."

Aboriginal paintings portray signs and symbols that reveal a profound understanding of the environment. Concentric circles depict water holes; other symbols were for rain and subterranean water. The mysterious symbols in the paintings of those closest to the land—the "original people"—serve as artful guides to nature's gifts, including the most precious, water. For Aborigines, a flock of birds is more than just a beautiful sight to behold. It is a sign that water lies nearby.

The growing concern all over the world for environmental conditions and pollution is something new. The problem has been there for over a century, but the awareness is new.

Isabel Allende

Applying lessons from the natives, the Holt family has learned to search the landscape for clues that will help them collect and store the outback's precious rain. Disclosing the secret of supplying his herd with water, Donald reveals his own understanding of the land in building dams to store precious rainfall. "Dams are a great asset to us. We read the country and see where the water runs, build the bank to create the dam, dig the hole, and catch the water. So a very small rain—even just 0.8 inch (20 millimeters)—can fill this dam. It's never been dry in 20 years, even in a series of bad droughts."

A keen awareness of the environment is providing the Holts with the tools they need to collect and store water. This kind of awareness needs to be cultivated in more and more places around the world. ■

From California to Kazakhstan. You can see the problem of droughts, the problem of disappearing lakes or rivers, shortages of water all over the place. It is really one of the greatest world problems. And I think the better part of it, the more promising is, we can handle it.

Shimon Peres

Interesting Facts . . .

- Aboriginal art dates back at least 30,000 years. In the paintings, straight lines depict routes traveled while wavy lines indicate rain or water.
- The government of Australia is beginning to view drought as a natural part of the climate cycle and is encouraging farmers to adopt policies that are sustainable in these conditions.
- Dating back to the Ice Age, Aborigine culture is the oldest in the world.

▪▪▪ Nets in the Mist— THE FOG CATCHERS OF CHUNGUNGO

IN THE EXTREME dryness of Chungungo, Chile, an ingenious use of a mysterious resource has helped the village get a handle on its chronic water problems.

Chungungo is a small fishing village located about 279 miles (450 kilometers) north of Santiago, huddled in the shadow of the coastal mountains. For decades, the 350 residents of Chungungo have lived with a chronic water shortage by transporting water over 30 miles (50 kilometers) in an old tanker truck once or twice a week. The cost of the water was high and the quality, suspect.

They have transformed completely the little village of Chungungo, which was totally lost because it was very underdeveloped and poor. There was no water and now the amount of water available per person has doubled.

Isabel Allende

In the mid-1980s, villagers working with Canadian developers devised a plan to mimic the action of the leaves on the town's eucalyptus trees. They reasoned that if the leaves could catch moisture, which in turn formed droplets, might not villagers construct nets which could likewise catch moisture?

Today, using huge plastic mesh nets, Chungungo fog collectors actually catch the fog and harvest the droplets. Dripping down the mesh, the water droplets fall into gutters. A pipeline then carries the water from the gutters down the mountain to tanks, and into the taps of homes and businesses of the village.

And what's more, the water is clean. The old system of delivering water by trucks often brought disease, as the trucks often carried other liquids in their tanks on other trips. The Camanchaga water has improved the health of the entire community. In addition to domestic consumption, Chungungo's fog collectors now provide enough water for about 10 acres (4 hectares) of community vegetable gardens. ■

In the northern part of Chile we have one of the driest deserts in the world. However, there is a climatic circumstance that is very favorable, something called the Camanchaga. It is a very heavy fog that comes usually with a cold wind. And they have developed a system, the Chileans, in conjunction with Canadians, a system to harvest the water from the fog.

Isabel Allende

Interesting Facts . . .

- One net structure measures 6 feet by 78 feet (2 meters by 24 meters) with a surface area of 58 square yards (48 square meters). These nets are now being used in 22 countries on six continents, such as Peru, Ecuador, Namibia, and South Africa.
- In Chungungo, 80 collectors provide 2,600 gallons (10,000 liters) of water per day to the village. Water consumption has increased from about 4 gallons (15 liters) per person, per day to 8.5 gallons (32 liters) per person, per day.
- The nets capture 30 percent of the water from the fog that passes through them. The entire system is operated purely on wind and gravity with no additional energy source needed.

■ ■ ■ Mexico City—A SINKING METROPOLIS

AT A TIME WHEN scarcity of quality water increases and huge costs are associated with filling the gap, inexpensive and practical solutions are stimulating interest in many areas of the world. Such innovative solutions to finding water are needed now more than ever.

Nowhere is this more evident than in Mexico City, the largest city in the world. It is a metropolis of 292 square miles (750 square kilometers), and home to nearly one-fifth of Mexico's population. Of all the difficult economic and social issues facing this sprawling complex of over 22 million people, the search for water has become the greatest challenge. Some even say that Mexico City is actually collapsing.

The historic city center has sunk 33 feet (10 meters) over the past 100 years. Its Grand Cathedral, the largest and oldest in Latin America, is supported by a steel corset while engineers battle to shore up its foundations. Buildings are slowly collapsing, streets rising and buckling, rail beds twisting, tracks bending. And all of it is connected to a water crisis that did not exist when the city came to life centuries ago.

In 1325, the wandering Mexican tribe known to us as Aztecs founded a great lagoon-city. According to legend, signs from a god directed them to establish

In terms of specific lessons that we might learn from the Nabataean systems, one that we are putting to use in various areas of the country is the absolute importance of preventing pollution, preventing contamination of drinking water. So we are trying to make use of a range of different approaches that may well reflect or mirror in some way how the Nabataeans set their priorities in the past.

Queen Noor of Jordan

their capital on thousands of acres (hectares) of marshlands near Lake Texcocco. Here they constructed a giant web of exotic floating gardens.

The small floating gardens of Xochimilco are all that remain of the great Aztec vision in today's Mexico City. Tourists and city residents cruise its waterways in brightly colored flat-bottom boats. The music of mariachi bands fills the air on a Sunday afternoon. The festive mood in this public park belies the destructive handling of the city's resources and its unprecedented water crisis.

Today, Mexico City depends on groundwater for 80 percent of its supply. Most of that water comes from the Mexico Valley aquifer. But the aquifer is not being recharged. An ever-expanding layer of asphalt and concrete is preventing rainwater from making its way back into the ground. Much of this rainwater is lost to evaporation. The depletion of the aquifer has caused a shifting and settling of the land. And the evidence is everywhere: crumbling roadways, cracked and burst pipes, precious water wasted.

This has become a place where, for millions of poor families, finding a clean glass of water has become a hollow dream. In the poor neighborhoods of the city, water comes through a tap only once a week. Sometimes it is clean, sometimes it is dirty. Residents spend a large portion of their meager income on bottled water.

But not all residents of Mexico City suffer from lack of water. The elite can afford water in abundance, for every domestic need, for gardens, for daily car washing, for recreation, and more. In fact, a mere 9 percent of the people in Mexico City use 75 percent of the city's total water supply. In view of such inequities, Mexico City's search for water must be a broad-based effort, beginning with a dramatic change in attitude.

Lessons from ancient peoples can be effective tools in shifting attitudes. Lessons that teach a keen understanding of the available resources and how to collect and preserve them. ■

Interesting Facts . . .

- Mexico City sits on a plateau approximately 7,000 feet (2,100 meters) above sea level. The altitude combined with a lack of regional water bodies make it impractical to import water to Mexico City.
- Mexico City gets most of its 28 inches (710 millimeters) of rainfall between the months of June and September.
- The aquifer under Mexico City has been declining by about 1 yard (1 meter) per year. Mexico City loses almost 40 percent of its water each year to evaporation and seepage as it passes through a crumbling distribution system.
- The World Health Organization has set a minimum standard of 39 gallons (150 liters) of water per day that should be available to domestic consumers. 19.5 gallons (75 liters) per day are necessary to protect against household diseases, and 13 gallons (50 liters) per person, per day are needed for basic sanitation. In the poor neighborhoods of Mexico City it is not uncommon to have to live on 5 gallons (20 liters) per day.

Water is the source of life for everyone.

The Dalai Lama

We take things for granted, like water. To have clean water and water coming out of the tap is like this God-given right.

Ted Danson

We have got delicious drinks coming from I don't know how many companies... but water is for me, especially when I'm thirsty, the best thing to drink. So for me, I like water.

Johan Cruyff

CHAPTER FOUR

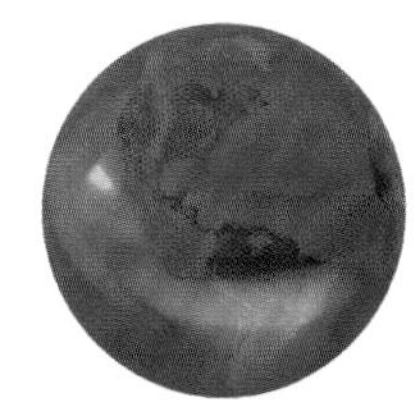

Our Daily Water

FROM DAILY NECESSITY to liquid extravagance, from simple chores to sports and recreation, water flows through the lives of every man, woman, and child on Earth.

Our need for daily water takes many forms. The most basic is biological. When pushed to the limit, we can survive for nearly a month without food. But without water, we may die in less than a week.

Man's biological engine cannot run without water. Water carries nutrients to our cells, and cellular waste to our kidneys. It regulates our body's temperature through perspiration. It serves as a shock absorber inside our eyes and spinal cord. It lubricates and cushions our joints. In times of peak performance, when every fiber demands precious fluid to power our body-engine, the need for water is greatest of all.

Each of us consumes 2 to 3 quarts (2 to 3 liters) of water every day. In turn, each day we exhale a third of a quart (0.3 liter) of water, sweat out half a quart (0.5 liter) of it, and expel another quart and a half (1.5 liters) of it.

Every human body is a small river, a steady flow of unseen water. That means 2.5 gallons (10 liters) of water flow through a family of four each day. For a city of 20 million, 13 million gallons (50 million liters) of water per day flow through its residents. And the world's population of 6 billion represents a daily flow of 4 billion gallons (15 billion liters) of water, six times the discharge of the Mississippi River.

But the water inside our bodies, and the amount required to replenish our biological needs, is simply one of the demands for daily water. Today, worldwide use of daily water varies greatly; from as low as 1 gallon (4 liters) of water per person, per day in some countries, to as high as 200 gallons (758 liters) of water per person, per day in others.

The explanation behind this great variance begins with where we live.

■ ■ ■ Valencia, Spain— LEARNING TO LIVE WITH DROUGHT

AN APARTMENT BLOCK in the city of Valencia, Spain, is home to the Ribella family. Like most families in Spain, a small river of water is delivered to their apartment through a connection from the municipal water system.

Domestic water use in Spain is about 100 gallons (380 liters) per person, per day. For years, the Ribellas have met their daily water needs with the simple touch of a faucet. But recent events have shown the Ribellas and their neighbors that their daily water supply is limited.

Beginning in 1990, periodic droughts in Spain became more serious and more prolonged. As a result, by 1995, more than ten million Spaniards—a quarter of the population—had to contend with water shortages. During the summer of 1999, those shortages grew so severe that local authorities imposed water rationing.

Rather than waiting for the situation to worsen, the Spanish government began education campaigns aimed at saving water. Using nationwide television, radio, and billboards, they began to change attitudes toward daily water use among families like the Ribellas.

Wherever in Spain we went to play tournaments at the end of the summer, there were all those restrictions on water. Which means, we don't spill it. If you take a shower—you've got to take a shower—but don't stand there 10 minutes.

Johan Cruyff

Today, the campaign promoting water conservation is reaching both homeowners and merchants all over Valencia. In this city, the combination of education, information, and water-saving products is helping to reduce the amount of daily water used throughout the community. Appliance stores are doing a great business selling water-efficient showers, faucets, toilets, and washing machines.

Each new water-efficient toilet can save a family up to 78 gallons (300 liters) of water per day. When multiplied by thousands of families in Valencia and millions more across Spain, that kind of savings is making a positive difference. Educational programs are beginning to change attitudes and individuals are changing habits. ■

Every human should have the idea of taking care of the environment, of nature, of water. So using too much or wasting water should have some kind of feeling or some kind of concern. Some sort of responsibility and with that, a sense of discipline.

The Dalai Lama

Interesting Facts . . .

- Within Spain's water network, about 60 percent of agricultural water is lost to leakage, and about 25 to 50 percent of domestic water is lost.
- New water-saving washing machines use only about 13 gallons (49 liters) per wash, compared to about 21 gallons (80 liters) per wash for older machines. New dishwashers can save almost 5 gallons (20 liters) of water per cycle. New efficient showerheads can save as much as 40 percent of the water used by older showers.

■ ■ ■ Windhoek, Namibia—NO WATER TO WASTE

Supply is relative and Valencia's limited supply seems abundant when compared to other areas of the world. With only 10 inches (250 millimeters) of rainfall per year, Namibia is the driest country south of the Sahara. Constant scarcity of water has shaped the attitudes of individuals all over Namibia, including the Lucas family.

At their home on the outskirts of Windhoek, the Lucas family knows that in this land of deserts and warm winds, even the tiniest amount of daily water must never be taken lightly. In this place of low rainfall, extreme temperatures, and strong seasonal winds, the daily water usage amounts to just over 1 gallon (4 liters) per person, per day.

The family has its daily water pumped from a reservoir by their landlord. Each day the Lucases and their four children share the same small basin of water for washing. Because the Lucases are aware of how much water they have at their disposal, they are very careful of how they use this water. For example, the tub of wash water is re-used in their outdoor toilet. Plants are watered with the water used to do the dishes. And for each additional use of daily water—for drinking, cooking, laundry—the Lucases must allocate their precious water carefully and efficiently. This family makes the best use of its available clean water by finding as many different uses for it as possible.

On a larger scale, the city of Windhoek is finding ways to use the same water over and over. Namibia is the only country in the world that purifies sewage water in a way that makes it potable, and then distributes it back to consumers.

As water passes through homes it is contaminated by detergents and human wastes. At the Gammams Wastewater Treatment Plant in Windhoek, raw sewage goes through a series of steps to make it potable again.

The first step in the process is separating coarse trash and rubbish using a series of screens and grilles. In an extended aeration procedure, colonies of pollution-eating bacteria are grown and begin to work. Ninety-nine percent of the bacteria is then removed in sedimentation tanks.

Our own body—what is it?—about 80 percent is water.

Johan Cruyff

Finally, using a technique called "ultra filtration," the water is forced through bundles of straws constructed of membranes so fine that all remaining bacteria and even viruses are filtered out of the water. Pesticides and chemicals are removed using a charcoal filtration process.

The whole operation takes about a week to turn sewage back into drinking water. These high-tech recycling processes are helping Windhoek meet its daily water needs by providing about one-third to one-half of the domestic water used in the city.

But due to the 5 percent annual population growth rate of the city, Windhoek has joined the rest of Namibia in developing educational programs to ensure that the whole country is as conscious of water as the Lucas family.

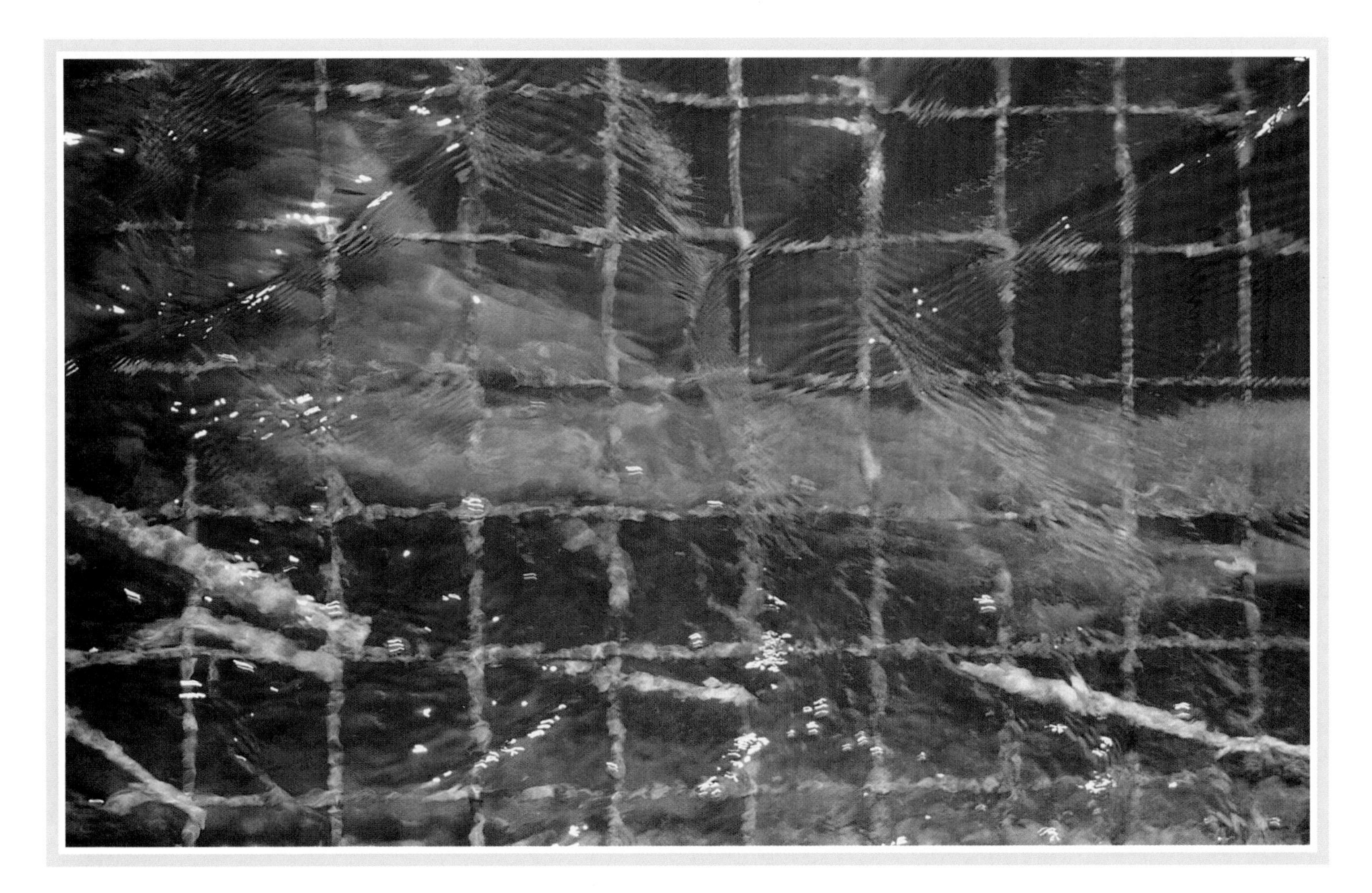

I have lived in countries where to wash your hair is a luxury, because there is so little water that you cannot think of wasting it washing your hair. And then I realize that I live in a place where I see the faucets open and the water just being wasted.

Isabel Allende

In school classrooms all over the country, teachers and water conservation experts have been working to develop good, practical attitudes toward the use and care of daily water supplies.

Currently, about 65,000 students each year learn the importance of water in their lives, and what to do to preserve water supplies for the future.

Children learn good water habits like turning off the tap while brushing their teeth. This simple action saves up to 3 quarts (3 liters) of water each time. When multiplied by the thousands of people in Windhoek, this adds up to considerable savings of a precious resource in a country that has no water to waste. ■

Lyrics to song sung by
Namibian School Children

Children of Namibia hear our cry...
You better save water or it will die.
We have a land that is so great...
We also have a problem we all hate.
The rains fall on dams, the rivers flow...
The cattle breed and the bushes grow.
Times are good and life is sweet.
Now let's talk about the things we know...
Not having any water is our biggest fault.
So, Children of Namibia hear our cry . . . "

I'm from Arizona where water was scarce. But then coming into California it feels like it's plentiful. I used to be kind of mindless about it. I love the sound of running water, I love long showers. So, I confess I'm not the best at this. But you educate yourself.

Ted Danson

Interesting Facts . . .

- From 1987 to 1997 Windhoek's population doubled, yet its water use remained at 1987 levels due to conservation efforts. But despite those efforts it is projected that the city will face severe water shortages by 2002 because of a rapidly growing population.
- Namibia is beginning to experiment with storing surface water underground to prevent large amounts of loss to evaporation when water is stored in reservoirs.

▪ ▪ ▪ Phoenix, Arizona— AN ARTIFICIAL AURA OF ABUNDANCE

BECAUSE OF THE SCARCITY of water in Namibia, ideas of conservation are more readily adopted than in some equally dry areas, where attitudes are much more difficult to change.

Phoenix, Arizona, has been called a Jewel in the Sunbelt. It is one of the fastest-growing cities in the United States. With about 7 inches (178 millimeters) of rainfall per year, the climate in Phoenix is actually drier than that of Windhoek. But attitudes toward daily water use in this booming Southwest city are very different from those of water-conscious Namibia.

The Guyette family of Phoenix uses an astonishing 780 gallons (3,000 liters) of water per day. This average suburban Phoenix family uses over 260,000 gallons (1 million liters) of water per year. A seemingly endless stream of water flows from a variety of faucets and fixtures.

Carefree attitudes about water in Phoenix are a result of a culture that has been disconnected from the natural limitations of geography and environment. Money has made a difference for Arizona—money that pays for transporting water from a distant source. The Central Arizona Project (C.A.P.) is a technological marvel that brings water from the distant Colorado River to the neighborhoods of Phoenix. This $4 billion conduit for daily water provides an illusion of plenty in a region of parched landscapes and a sinking groundwater table.

Ironically, the very technology that has allowed water to be diverted to this desert metropolis has had both positive and negative results. The ability to import surface water from the Colorado River and deliver it as daily water for homes and businesses has helped to prevent regional environmental damage from continued pumping of groundwater aquifers.

But the wonder and efficiency of C.A.P., as its Colorado River water rolls down through the desert, has deprived Mexico of water downstream. It has also led many people in Arizona and California to view daily water as an unlimited resource.

More than 25 million people currently drink Colorado River water on a daily basis. Cities like Las Vegas and Los Angeles also depend on this river for their daily water needs. Officials from many of these cities are beginning to recognize that the Colorado is not in fact an unlimited supply of water. As the region's population grows they realize that attitudes toward the use of water must change.

So, I'm no different than anyone else. I have a tinge of guilt about how much I use. And a little more awareness of how precious water is and how it will become, unfortunately, what we fight over.

Ted Danson

In Arizona, C.A.P. and its controlling body, the Central Arizona Water Conservation District, is part of a statewide program to change individual attitudes toward daily water. Similar to the education program in Namibia, school children in Phoenix are involved in programs to create new awareness of the need to conserve water.

Xeriscape® technology, landscaping with low-water-use plants, is a prime example of how individuals can become part of the solution to problems of daily water usage. In Phoenix, a state-of-the-art demonstration garden symbolizes new public resolve to address nature's warning about water scarcity. Xeriscape® plants use just one-tenth of the water that a lawn of green grass uses.

Each lawn that is replaced with Xeriscape® plants saves 260 gallons (1,000 liters) of water per day. This can add up to huge savings as millions of people in this vast region become aware of the value of this resource. ■

Interesting Facts . . .

- The term Xeriscape® was first used in 1978 in Denver, Colorado. It means "water conservation through creative landscaping," and is a registered trademark of the Denver Water Board.
- A well-designed Xeriscape® landscape can reduce yard maintenance by as much as 50 percent. Xeriscape® landscaping needs less fertilizers and pesticides thus helping the environment.
- You can save 30 to 50 percent on your water bill with an efficient lawn irrigation system. Between 10 a.m. and 4 p.m., about 65 percent of water sprinkled on lawns evaporates.
- Over half the water used in the Phoenix area is for landscaping. Mulching can reduce the need for water by as much as 40 percent.

Unfortunately, water has become such a luxury in many places that there is a price for it. I do not agree with that, I think that water should be available to everyone free, but rationed. You should be very aware of how much water you can use per day, per person.

Isabel Allende

The notion that a few people can own resources is so frightening a concept. Because the ownership is about economic ownership and it's not for the value of the community. It's about how a few people can be made richer.

Anita Roddick

CHAPTER FIVE

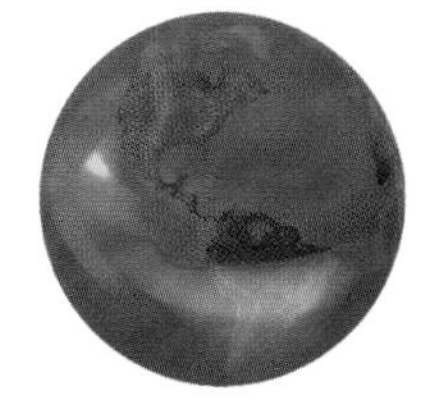

A Price to Pay

WHEREVER WATER IS SCARCE, the growing demand means that aging delivery systems are inadequate to meet current needs. Upgrading the water infrastructure of even a small town is a monumental task. Miles and miles of pipe, hours and hours of labor, heavy equipment for excavating—all bleed off municipal financial resources.

Whether the responsibility of delivering water falls into public or private hands is the source of raging debate. Some argue that private companies are more efficient and can better serve the needs of growing communities. Others contend that water is a public resource, a basic need, and that it is wrong for this basic need to be in private hands and subject to the fluctuations of the private marketplace.

How much money people pay for water is also a source of controversy. Whether it is farmers or homeowners who have to pay, the price affects their attitudes. Many communities subsidize the effort that delivers inexpensive water to homes. It has been argued that subsidized water from municipalities devalues the resource and leads to a false sense of abundance and a lack of concern for the resource. The idea that charging money for water encourages conservation, and respect for the resource is being tested in many parts of the world.

Whether putting a price on water is considered a problem or a solution, the reality today is that in rural areas, towns, and urban centers—virtually everywhere that people use water—there is a price to pay. The issues concerning the setting of a fair and equitable price for water are complex, and no single solution works for all places. In fact, each community must decide for itself how it will transport and pay for its water.

■ ■ ■ The Water Bearers of Ajmer—
FREE WATER AT A PRICE

THE FORTRESS CITY of Ajmer is a bustling Islamic enclave in the midst of India's Hindu culture. Located at the foot of the Aravalis Mountains in the Rajasthan Province, Ajmer, "the invincible hill," is the former stronghold of the great Chaunhan rulers.

For over a thousand years, citizens of Ajmer have paid for a simple and vital service, a service performed by the *bhistee*, the bearers of fresh water. Several times daily, they draw water for their livelihood. Often climbing to dizzying heights, they transport their precious cargo in hand-sewn goatskins, called *masaks*.

Delivering water to the mosques, the *bhistee* charge a modest fee, calculated strictly on the distance and height carried. Payment is for the delivery alone, not for the water itself.

"Putting a price tag on water... Oh, how the ancient ones would have cringed. Allah has given us water, it is free for all," proclaim many Islamic Mullahs (religious teachers). In many areas of the world, faithful Muslims still wash their hands, feet and face before entering the mosque, with water that is free, but growing more scarce by the day.

In fact, water transportation is usually the driving force behind setting a price for water. It costs money to build and maintain water delivery systems. But although reliable water delivery at a reasonable price still exists for many, concerns about costs are growing. Some are concerned that in many parts of the world, the modern water carriers are now large, private, for-profit corporations. ■

You know the Lord gave us fresh air free of charge. So we waste it, we pollute it, we kill it, we don't understand the value of it. We pay for tomatoes, so when it comes to tomatoes we are very careful, we wash it, we pack it, we put it in the refrigerator. When it comes to fresh water, you know, it's so normal and natural that people are wasting it and destroying it.

Shimon Peres

Interesting Facts . . .

- The Rajasthan Province of India has recently undergone a period of severe drought. As a form of relief, the government has begun providing free diesel fuel for trucks to carry water.
- In this province people have begun to build tanks to capture rainwater. Five hours of heavy rain can fill a 10,000-gallon (40,000-liter) tank, which can provide enough water for 50 children for an entire year.

■ ■ ■ Britain's Private Water Companies—THE GREAT EXPERIMENT

Putting waterways in the hands of private companies to be run as a for-profit operation raises questions. The questions are more about who owns the water—municipalities or private companies—and how they determine and collect the fees. These questions are highly debated.

Great Britain has come to wide-scale privatization of water after years of floundering governmental control. From picture-postcard villages to large British cities, the waterworks of old are no longer working. There have always been private water companies throughout the country. But water was managed mainly by Britain's ten state-run Water Boards, whose ancient systems had crumbled by the late 1980s, creating an opportunity for private companies. In 1989 the government sold its ten Water Boards to private corporations.

The shift to privatization of water was a shock to many long-time Water Board customers. For the first time ever, someone was making a profit out of their most basic need, water.

Although emotions run high about privatization, the water companies have had to spend huge sums on repairs and improvements throughout Great Britain. And as upgrading costs continue to rise, European law has also imposed new wastewater regulations on water companies, resulting in still more expenditure. For instance, one company that serves a large coastal area is spending billions on updating treatment procedures and pipes. They are replacing an out-dated sewage system that allowed raw sewage to be dumped into the sea. The new system will discharge only treated water that is as clean as natural river water.

The subjects of the United Kingdom no longer own the waterways. It used to be an inalienable right to own the waterways, as all subjects should. So now companies have come in—they privatize the water, say that there's an economic value to that water, and sell that water to the highest bidder.

Anita Roddick

These improvements have a positive impact on the environment, but the costs are being passed along to disgruntled customers.

In the first decade of water privatization, Britain wrestled with many problems, such as tough penalties levied against customers who do not pay their bills. In 1991, soon after privatization began, some 21,000 homes were disconnected from their water supply for non-payment of bills.

Many people viewed such stringent measures as ruthless. As a result, legislation now protects many water customers. A government watchdog organization now influences the price of water, to ensure an appropriate balance between the cost to water companies for repairs, maintenance, and upgrading, and the cost to consumers.

The major investment period for Britain's private water companies is now over, and most are reducing water bills to clients. In addition, the Drinking Water Inspectorate ensures that water companies supply their customers with high-quality water.

Quality water and a cleaner environment come at a price, to be sure. Whether that price should be paid to governments or corporations is still being debated, not only in Great Britain, but all over the world. ■

Interesting Facts . . .

- By 1999 the water companies of the U.K. had invested nearly $50 billion (over £33 billion) in water systems serving over 20 million people.
- From 1989 to 1999 the number of swimmable beaches in England and Wales increased from 401 to 463.
- Between 1989 and 1996, the average cost of household water and sewage services nearly doubled, but the latest round of price regulation by the government oversight agency has targeted a 12-percent price reduction.
- Now that the government is not in the sewage business, its regulatory agencies are better equipped to regulate. There have been over 200 prosecutions of water companies in recent years.

■ ■ ■ Mirzapur, India— REBUILDING A GOVERNMENT SYSTEM

WHILE THE SOLUTION to Great Britain's failed municipal control of water was privatization, it is not the answer for everyone. Some municipalities are working hard to solve their internal problems so that water systems can remain in the public domain.

Mirzapur, India, is a bustling city on the Ganges River, a city wrestling with the relics of a system for water delivery dating back to British colonization, and a municipal coffer that has run dry.

Municipal records were in turmoil and many residents were not even registered. This made collecting taxes impossible. Without a sufficient revenue source, the stream of water to Mirzapur residents was severely disrupted. Only middle-class home owners and areas with political clout received water—40 percent of Mirzapur's population had no water connection at all. Many of these people had to pay up to 20 percent of their income to private water vendors, with no guarantee that the water was safe. Because of the high cost of private water, many people used small pumps to tap into the system illegally.

With illegal taps draining an already crumbling system and no money for maintenance, let alone new construction, the municipality was severely handicapped. Determined to maintain public control of water, the municipality brought in American engineering consultant Scott Gibbons to assess the situation.

Gibbons recalls that even more than the water infrastructure, the government infrastructure needed an overhaul. "The Mirzapur municipality was bankrupt, so the most important thing was to get control of the municipal administrative records. We had to computerize thousands of property records. We had to create the property maps for the entire city. From this we were able to create the first municipal Geographic Information System (GIS) in India. Now, the Mirzapur GIS provides a powerful tool to the municipality to regain control over its property and water tax records.

"Because the municipality couldn't even pay the current staff salaries, the new revenues that are coming in will first be used to pay the salaries. That's the most important thing, because once the salaries are paid the employees are much more likely to do good work and to respond to the directions of their supervisors."

With motivated workers, good records, and the revenue from equitable taxation, improvements were made to the systems of water delivery and quality. Even the poorest areas of Mirzapur are now served.

Gaining access to the precious resource of water has not only inspired residents to work to ensure the safety of their drinking water, but has also revived their sense of dignity. With guidance from non-governmental organizations, communities like Mirzapur have been rewarded for taking responsibility for correcting systemic problems with continued public control of the water infrastructure. ■

The population is growing all the time. The water resources were not properly handled, or properly planned, and clearly not enriched. The running of the water is in old systems and in old pipes. As I say again, there is a great price for the lack of modern ways to irrigate or to conduct the water.

Shimon Peres

Interesting Facts . . .

- In 1997 property tax bills were sent out for the first time in seventeen years. From 1996 to 1998 tax revenues in Mirzapur rose 42 percent.
- The average income for a family of five in Mirzapur is 2,009 rupees ($43, £30) per month.
- Even with low incomes, residents of one poor community in India raised money to help pay for a hand pump and a street drain. When the government could not send sweepers to clean the new drain, community members opted to protect their investment and clean it themselves.

Santiago, Chile— A GLOBAL BUSINESS OPPORTUNITY

MANY MUNICIPALITIES have chosen another solution to their water problems, involving rich, private multinational companies. In contrast to many developing cities, Santiago provides almost 100 percent of its population with clean drinking water, but a mere 2 percent of its sewage water is treated. Vast quantities of wastewater are discharged directly onto the streets, flowing into rivers and gorges without having undergone any type of monitoring or treatment.

In 1999, a large French and Spanish water management company was selected to manage the water supply and develop wastewater services for the 44 districts of Santiago. The multinational company is planning to make dramatic changes to pollution problems. New sewage treatment facilities are being designed. These facilities and the connections to them will be expensive. Community water bills will have to increase to pay for the construction.

There is a reality. And the reality is that there is overpopulation and the resources are limited. So obviously water is priced—and sometimes very highly—depending on where it is. In most cities it is priced highly and that will happen more and more. We have to be aware of it and accept it as one of the awful things of life. I hope that air will not be also rationed and paid for.

Isabel Allende

While the cost of water will rise, the cleaner water will save the community money in medical treatments for people who have suffered from contact with polluted water. The calculations are complex and no one knows just how much the price of water will rise. Many residents share the view that something needs to be done; yet there are still concerns to be addressed.

The views of one Santiago resident express this concern. "The newspapers have printed that EMOS, a subsidiary of the French water company, will increase the price of the water. That increase in price will be used to decontaminate the waters of the rivers of Santiago. This increase in the price will be used to finance the building of the sewage treatment plants in Santiago. I think it's a good thing, but it will sure have an impact on the budget of the poor people."

How to supply the poor with water under a private multinational system is still a source of public debate. As water becomes an international business, questions of who will monitor fair pricing practices on an international scale remain largely unanswered. ■

If there is one area where equity is crucial and essential, I think it should be on the issue of water.
Kofi Annan

Interesting Facts . . .

- The French and Spanish consortium acquired 42 percent of Santiago's water company for $957 million (£657 million).
- The French part of the water company is currently providing 77 million people with drinking water and 52 million people with wastewater services in such diverse places as Atlanta, Manila, Casablanca, and Sydney.
- Some estimate the potential of the global water market to be $300 billion (£200 billion) per year.

I think the farmers in our countries—
because of economic pressures—
are becoming more efficient every year.

Jimmy Carter

Increasing global population has put a lot of pressure on the need for water.

Kofi Annan

From less and less land and from less and less water, you can have more and more products, more and more results.

Shimon Peres

CHAPTER SIX

The Aorta of Agriculture

FOR HUMAN AND ANIMAL survival, there is an unquestionable need for clean water. People need to drink. The other undeniable need is for food. People need to eat. And in order to have food, there must be water—a great deal of it. In fact, by most estimates, agriculture uses as much as 75 percent of our global fresh water supply.

Across thousands of fields, paddies, and terraces, in greenhouses and backyard plots, water is the aorta of agriculture, carrying the lifeblood to crops that will feed the world's people and livestock. It is by far the largest user of fresh water.

"Farming" is people and plants in harmony. Digging the soil, planting. It is a process common to all cultures. And whether it's a small family garden or a sprawling agri-business, the unifying force in that harmony is, was, and always will be—water.

From cotton to corn, in days gone by, irrigation seemed to be the key to successful agriculture. But now, as overexploitation of existing fresh water reservoirs is becoming a problem, present methods of irrigation are being reconsidered.

▪▪▪ Rice—FEEDING THE WORLD WITH WATER

THROUGHOUT the twentieth century, irrigation has been considered the answer to many water uncertainties in agriculture. In Asia, more than 80 percent of the available fresh water is used for irrigation, and 90 percent of irrigation water is used for one crop, rice.

Rice is the basic food for billions of people. In Japan, and elsewhere, it is also at the core of modern life. From sake to rice-paper furnishings, both culturally and economically, rice remains a constant factor in all of Asian life.

Rice is also a heavy consumer of water. It takes an average of 650 gallons (2,500 liters) of water to produce 1 pound (0.45 kilogram) of rice. In places like Bali, farmers follow the tradition of flooding rice fields as a method of weed control. But over the last hundred years, Asia has been facing a dramatically increasing

One consideration on a global scale that hasn't been adequately addressed is not just the allocation of water to a big city or to the farms nearby, where there is competition. But how do you conserve water, how do you make the use of it more efficient? Because there is not going to be an increase in total supplies.

Jimmy Carter

demand to feed a rapidly growing population. This ever-increasing demand leads to an inevitable conclusion: future rice production must focus on far more efficient irrigation systems and reduced water consumption by the rice plant itself.

At the International Research Center for Agricultural Sciences in Ibaraki, Japan, development continues on a new strain of water-efficient, drought-resistant, bug-proof rice, known as "dry rice." It is a very adaptable type of rice. It can be grown in rotation with other crops, and it is more drought resistant and weed resistant than any other type of rice. With this approach, fields no longer have to be flooded continuously by irrigation in order to protect and nurture transplanted rice seedlings.

The extent to which pesticides will be needed in this process remains to be seen. And only time will tell if dry rice will be embraced by the marketplace. This experiment is only the beginning of the race to grow more food with less water. It is a challenge needing all members of society to be receptive to new ideas and technologies. ■

We have the problem all over the world and as the population expands there is need for more food. Managing [water] and using it responsibly is essential—or there's not going to be enough for everyone.

Kofi Annan

Interesting Facts . . .

- Rice is half the daily diet for one out of three people on the planet. Each year there are an additional 80 million to 100 million mouths to feed.
- Ninety percent of the world's rice is grown and consumed in Asia. The United States is the third largest exporter of rice behind Thailand and Vietnam. Twenty-five percent of all the rice produced in the U.S. is grown in California.
- Between 1900 and 1990, water usage by the human race increased at twice the rate of the population increase.
- Projections suggest that most Asian countries will have severe water problems by the year 2025.

■ ■ ■ Beef—IT'S WATER FOR DINNER

AS WE ENTER the twenty-first century, farmers who grow different staple crops in other parts of the world face similar challenges.

Southwest Kansas is at the heart of America's high plains region. On a warm summer evening a festive country barbecue celebrates the prime agricultural product that supports so many in this land, beef.

The key to everything in this farm country—including beef—is water. In fact, the raising of beef uses up 30 percent of the total agricultural water supply, and the demand for beef worldwide is growing. The connection between water and high-quality Kansas beef is one all-important crop, corn.

Across America's high plains, the struggle for water to nurture crops spans many generations. Some farmers, like Melvin Winger, can still remember the droughts of the 1930s that ruined their crops. "It was all dry land, farmed, mostly wheat. And it didn't rain near as much. We didn't have fertilizer. We didn't have a lot of things we have now. So we didn't raise very much, and it was just kind of sustaining ourselves."

Relief came in the late 1930s, when farmers drilling for water discovered the Ogallala Aquifer. An aquifer is a huge underground reservoir of water. The discovery of this aquifer allowed farmers to irrigate on a grand scale.

Seas of corn now sustain a huge agricultural economy. From the sky you can see large circular irrigation patterns spreading out across the southwestern Kansas landscape. From the ground, the source is just as visible. Giant center-pivot arms reach for over half a mile (1 kilometer), delivering water to thirsty cornfields.

But irrigation is not without complications. Pesticides and fertilizers pollute the irrigation water that passes through fields. In addition, much of the water sprayed high into the air by old-style high-pressure sprinklers is lost to evaporation. And the waste of irrigation water on such a large scale threatens to dry out these vast oceans of grain.

For too long, southwestern Kansas farmers have been mining aquifer water to meet the demands of agri-business without considering the consequences of continually exceeding the recharge rate. Like most aquifers, Ogallala's recharge comes directly from rain falling on the soil and seeping below. When the amount of water withdrawn from an aquifer continually exceeds the recharge, nature's underground tank begins running low.

When I was President, which is now twenty years ago, one of our constant debates was the allocation of water, primarily for irrigation. And, of course, farmers and city people have now begun to contend for limited supplies of water. Is a gallon of water going to go to Los Angeles to let people water lawns, or is it going to be sidetracked into previously desert areas for irrigation purposes to grow our food? That's the basic question, and it is becoming increasingly a subject of lawsuits and arguments in our Congress, and decisions made by our President. Who is going to get the increasingly scarce supplies of water?

Jimmy Carter

Today, farmers young and old realize that the time for action is now. America's heartland, and world markets, cannot afford to have this depletion continue. Through the Western Kansas Irrigation Research Project, Kansas State University is helping farmers reduce their rate of water use and prolong the life of the Ogallala Aquifer.

Researchers are testing different types of low-level, high-efficiency nozzle heads. This precision system will allow farmers to deliver irrigation directly to the plants, preventing the loss of large amounts of water to evaporation.

Although far more work must be done to preserve water, these combined efforts have begun to move large agri-business operations toward becoming more sustainable providers of food for a growing global population. ■

You know the problem is that agriculture depends upon the Lord in Heaven and the Farmer on Earth. It is a joint venture. But one of the partners is totally unreliable; I mean, the holy partner brings in droughts and brings in cold, brings in heat, and what not. So we—the human beings—must be much more coordinated and understanding, if we don't want to become a victim of a cruel nature.

Shimon Peres

Interesting Facts . . .

- It takes 24 gallons (91 liters) of water to produce 1 pound (453 grams) of edible potatoes. It takes 182 gallons (689 liters) of water to produce 1 pound (453 grams) of corn.
- One bushel (35 liters) of corn produces 5.6 pounds (2.5 kilograms) of beef. In 1999 the average person consumed 69 pounds (31 kilograms) of beef.
- Livestock consumes 70 percent of U.S. grain production.
- The Ogallala Aquifer covers an area of about 225,000 square miles (585,000 square kilometers).
- Brazil estimates that 38 percent of its rainforest was destroyed for cattle pasture.

■ ■ ■ Drip Irrigation in Kenya—LOW-TECH, SMALL FARMS

IN KENYA, East Africa, the environment is fragile, financial means are limited, and rainfall is minimal. Just 250 miles (400 kilometers) from the capital city of Nairobi is Kenya's Rift Valley Province. Farmers working small plots in the districts of Marakwet and Keiyo contend regularly with drought.

Despite these uncertainties, nearly every adult in these two districts is employed in agriculture. And, in spite of drought, food production continues as it has for centuries.

Throughout the world the methods of irrigation vary, mostly depending on financial means and geographic location. Despite the enormous waste of their precious resource of water and the washing away of fertile topsoil, wild flooding and furrow irrigation are practiced by many farmers according to old traditions.

But others have found new solutions to water scarcity. Some have begun lining furrows with cement to prevent water from seeping into the ground en route to fields. In Keiyo, farmers are being helped by a technique known as drip irrigation.

As the name suggests, drip irrigation is the drop-by-drop localized application of water from a grid just above the soil surface. Drip irrigation systems can reduce water use by 30 to 70 percent while increasing yields by 20 to 90 percent. While drip irrigation is helping small farms in many areas of the world, it is also being applied to large operations. ■

With new technology, which is able to regulate the amount of water one uses to irrigate, we may not have to use as much water or waste as much water as we do now. But it's a matter of education and preparing those who do not have that knowledge to be able to get it, and work with them to implement it and help save water.

Kofi Annan

Interesting Facts . . .

- Irrigation accounts for two-thirds of global water use, but less than half of that water reaches the roots of plants. With drip irrigation, 85 to 90 percent of the water reaches the plant roots.
- Each year the world's farmers are pumping 216 billion cubic yards (160 billion cubic meters) more water than is being recharged by rainfall.
- Importing about a ton of wheat is the same as importing about 1,000 tons of water.

Dutch Tomatoes—HIGH-TECH, BIG BUSINESS

DEVELOPED IN ISRAEL, computerized irrigation has been exported. In these facilities minimal amounts of water are generating vast yields of vegetables.

Greenhouses in the Netherlands are a good example of maximizing water conservation by combining high technology with Mother Nature's gift of rain. Rainwater is collected from the roof of the greenhouse and transported to two large water basins of 13,000 cubic yards (10,000 cubic meters) each. In a high-tech version of the small farms in Kenya, the greenhouse is divided into several water-tap zones.

All of the irrigation pipes are connected to a central computer that feeds measured water through them. A pair of scales with plants on them measures the amount of water that is needed by gauging the weight of the plant. The computer takes care of the water supply of each individual plant, so each individual plant has its own water irrigation system.

Drip irrigation allows farmers to supply fertilizer to plants mixed in with water in a process known as "fertigation." This way the plant absorbs the fertilizer directly with the water. Any little excess water that drains off is collected and re-used in a closed-loop system, so the fertilizer does not migrate into the surrounding ecosystem.

One greenhouse covers about 11 acres (4.5 hectares) and grows 140 pounds (63 kilograms) of tomatoes every square yard or meter. Techniques like drip irrigation suggest that we can conserve water and maintain high crop yields. But all this technology assumes farmers have access to at least modest sources of clean water. ■

You know, in our case almost all irrigations are computerized. We have our own system of irrigation, the drop irrigation or the drip irrigation—you put water like a doctor puts some medicine in your eye, very very carefully.
Shimon Peres

Interesting Facts . . .

- Agricultural output in Israel over the past 30 years has increased almost 500 percent with very little increase in the amount of water used.
- In recent years North American greenhouse production of tomatoes has increased 90 percent.
- The Netherlands exports almost half its tomatoes to Germany.
- Between 1993 and 1997 Dutch tomato exports to the U.S. rose 379 percent.

■ ■ ■ *Aguas Negras*—IRRIGATION IN MEXICO

IN SOME PARTS of the world, supplies of clean water are not adequate to meet the immediate needs of local farmers. To sustain their farms and the people who depend on them for food, these growers have adopted the highly controversial reuse of wastewater.

In Irraputo, in the Mezquital Valley of Mexico, dwellers of this dry region have depended on "second-hand" water as the saving grace for their fields. In 1945, Mexico's Ministry of Agriculture and Water Resources established the Mezquital Irrigation District to manage distribution of Mexico City's *aguas negras,* "black waters," for irrigating the Mezquital Valley.

Today, the Mezquital Valley is the largest area in the world where wastewater is used for irrigation. A network of canals serves 222,000 acres (90,000 hectares) of farmland and their two main crops of alfalfa and maize. The drawback is that wastewater irrigation is not completely safe. In fact, many believe it to be highly unsanitary and dangerous to people's health.

In an attempt to protect the public's health, growing vegetables and fruits that could be eaten raw is prohibited by legislation. Some farmers use *aguas negras* only at the beginning of the season to get a head start on the competition.

Since the contamination of many types of vegetables by wastewater has caused serious gastrointestinal diseases, Mexico's National Water Commission is no longer leaving quality control up to canal operators and gate openers, as was the case for years.

The Commission is now redesigning its approach to second-hand-water irrigation to include a more specific quality-monitoring system for improving health standards for growing food, now and in the future. Mexico's struggle to provide cleaner, safer water to feed its vast population is a symptom of a problem we are facing on a global scale. ■

Interesting Facts . . .

- The Mezquital Valley's population grew from 350,000 in 1900 to 3 million by 1950. Today over 20 million people live in the region.
- Approximately 57 percent of the sewage in Mexico City is from domestic sources, and roughly 43 percent is from industrial sources.
- Only 7 percent of the wastewater flowing out of Mexico City is treated.
- Wastewater is irrigating over 3.2 million acres (1.33 million hectares) of farmland in China.

We do not sit down and treat this as an ecosystem. We break it up into little places.

Ted Danson

The Uzbekis have a saying: "If you run out of water, you run out of life."

Mikhail Gorbachev

But it's a tough trade-off in the sense that often the governments feel pressure to do something—to avoid future floods, to get water for irrigation, to be able to feed their population. But at the same time, they have to be careful not to damage the environment.

Kofi Annan

CHAPTER SEVEN

The Way of the River

"TIME IS A RIVER," wrote poet Jorge Luis Borges. "Time is a river which carries me along, but I *am* the river." It has ever been so for mankind. From the headwaters of the Euphrates, to the delta of the Rhine, we see much of ourselves and our destiny in the timeless flow of rivers.

Providing food and water, rivers were a natural place for nomadic peoples to settle down. Western civilization was nurtured between the banks of the Tigris and the Euphrates. Villages grew into cities using rivers as transportation highways. The great cities in the world have great rivers running through them.

But in settling on the banks of rivers, people have also put themselves in harm's way. Throughout history, countless people have been swept away by the raging liquid currents. Rivers have taught us about both the bounty and the burden of water.

The lessons of rivers have inspired visions of controlling their endless, but uneven, flow. We learned to dam them and divert them. We figured out how to take water from them to nurture our fields, and take energy from them to power our factories and light our cities. Yet, throughout the past century, harnessing rivers to meet our immediate need has often led to unforeseen and long-term consequences.

The Nile—BLESSING AND CURSE OF EGYPT

THE NILE is the world's longest river—4,136 miles (6,671 kilometers)—bound for the Mediterranean Sea. Traveling through Ancient Egypt, the Nile annually became a great brown rushing torrent, which peaked from September through October. In its wake came the gift of sediment, gathered from the Ethiopian highlands, swirled into a rich, thick black mud. These deposits were a boon to farmers throughout the Nile Valley.

For 3,000 years, the mighty Nile shaped nearly every facet of Egyptian life. Its sediment replenished the land. Its waters fed irrigation trenches and canals necessary to the growth of crops. Some scholars believe that the concept of "astrology" arose out of the need to accurately predict the time and locations of the annual Nile flood. For just as the Nile River could bring growth and prosperity, it could snatch them away in devastating fashion.

By the twentieth century, Egypt had taken steps toward controlling the great river, making its gifts predictable and abundant. With the help of the British, Egyptians built the Aswan Dam in 1902. In the early 1960s, Egyptian President Gamal Abdul Nasser fostered the engineering of the Aswan High Dam, a massive structure located about 3.5 miles (6 kilometers) north of the old Aswan Dam.

Today, the Aswan High Dam's hydroelectric equipment provides about half of all Egypt's electric power. Its massive walls help control the flooding of the Nile River, and man-made Lake Nasser provides a controlled flow of water in dry years. The Nile valley now yields several harvests each year instead of just one. As a result, Egypt's agricultural income has increased by 200 percent over the past thirty years.

Yet, for all its benefits, the Aswan High Dam has ushered in as many problems as it has solutions. The project flooded many rare archaeological sites and forced the removal of priceless monuments from Egypt's past—at a cost of over $40 million (£27.5 million).

Thousands of Nubean farm families were resettled, while their homes and culture were drowned beneath Lake Nasser. Containment of the Nile at the Aswan High Dam has drastically reduced the flow of silt and sand to the Nile delta, resulting in fewer nutrients for croplands. Artificial fertilizers must now be used to replace missing natural nutrients—fertilizers that add to the pollution of groundwater and the Nile.

Less water flowing downstream from the great dam has increased erosion of the shoreline, and allowed salt from the Mediterranean Sea to creep inland, making soil and groundwater abnormally salty.

Diseases such as Rift Valley cattle fever, malaria, and elephantiasis are an effect of the reduced flow and stagnant water pools. As a result, chlorine must now be added to drinking water to prevent widespread illness.

Most ominous of all, pressure from the sheer volume of water at Lake Nasser, leading to cracks in the High Dam, has caused seepage to surrounding dry land. If the dam should break, millions of people downstream would be killed and thousands of acres or hectares of croplands ruined.

Seeking a better life, modern-day Egyptians have harnessed the Nile. But that achievement is not without cost. Environmental and social problems are inevitable consequences when altering the flow of a mighty river. ■

The Nile united Egypt. It is said that the Nile is the gift of nature to Egypt. And that it has decided the nature of Egypt for generations and generations.

Shimon Peres

Interesting Facts . . .

- The Nile discharges 780,000 gallons (3 million liters) per second into the Mediterranean Sea.
- In the Mediterranean, sardines lived on nutrients from the Nile discharge. The sardine catch in the Mediterranean declined from 18,000 tons in 1962 to 600 tons in 1969 as the Aswan High Dam neared completion.
- Lake Nasser is the third largest reservoir in the world at 298 miles (480 kilometers) long and 10 miles (16 kilometers) wide. It holds 218 billion cubic yards (168 billion cubic meters) of water.
- Irrigation from Lake Nasser has turned 1.9 million acres (772,000 hectares) of desert into farmland.

■ ■ ■ The Aral Sea—DRAINING THE BLOOD OF A NATION

STARK WHITE FIELDS. Salt-covered shorelines. Long-abandoned boats strewn about on sandy waves of endless desert. Here, relics of past prosperity offer mute testimony to one of the world's greatest environmental disasters. The Aral Sea is a vast inland lake bisecting the republics of Kazakhstan and Uzbekistan. Originally it was the size of the entire country of Ireland. For centuries, the Amu-Dar'ya and Syr-Dar'ya rivers had provided the Aral Sea with constant fresh water, enriching its mineral composition and promoting diverse marine life.

Fifty years ago, in an effort to bolster Russia's textile industry, Russian Premiere Nikita Khrushchev ordered the diversion of water from the Amu-Dar'ya and Syr-Dar'ya rivers to the "white gold" fields, the cotton farms of Uzbekistan. Unlined and open ditch

I dealt a lot with water problems, including the problem concerning the distribution of water from the rivers Amu-Dar'ya and Syr-Dar'ya. The inhabitants of this region are confronted with an extremely pressing water problem that has had negative effects on the fate of the Aral Sea.

Mikhail Gorbachev

methods used to irrigate Uzbekistan's cotton fields led to wide-scale inefficiencies. Fully 80 percent of the water diverted from the Amu-Dar'ya and Syr-Dar'ya rivers for cotton farming was lost to evaporation and seepage. From the very beginning, Khrushchev's decision to divert this life-giving flow caused problems. The Aral Sea began to shrink, and its salinity increased.

Today, half of the Aral Sea has been lost. It is a loss of monumental proportions. With the Aral Sea drying up, and cotton farmers struggling to produce acceptable yields, a crisis began to affect some 30 million people all across Central Asia. In the early 1950s, the Aral Sea's commercial fishing industry was flourishing. It provided 60,000 people with jobs, homes, and a thriving, comfortable community life. Today, that industry is gone. Those who lived through the tragedy are haunted by bittersweet memories.

With more than 7,800 square miles (20,000 square kilometers) of salty, barren sea floor exposed, up to 43 million tons of contaminated dust is carried each year by winds and deposited on croplands and populated areas. In a region now gripped with poverty, children dig salt for money. But even the meager amounts of salt that they mine with their hands is a toxic menace, loaded with pesticides used in agriculture.

Well, these kinds of things are becoming evident on a spotty basis. A problem here, a problem way over there. And in the next couple of years other problems in between. So I think the inevitable trend is to have more and more local crises that begin to overlap until major political entities—World Bank, IMF, the United Nations, and others, and even maybe the Security Council of the United Nations—will have to be involved in some form for the allocation of the water supplies.

Jimmy Carter

With the collapse of the Soviet Union, the future of the Aral Sea and those who live there now rests with the central Asian republics in the Amu-Dar'ya and Syr-Dar'ya river basins. These republics are seeking help from international institutions, organizations with expertise in water management. A European-sponsored consulting firm is experimenting with ways to boost crop yields while reducing water usage. Until recently, Uzbeki cotton growers have used 4 to 5 times as much water as their counterparts in other nations. New programs are already aiming at cutting that usage in half.

Farm restructuring and reforms are only beginning to improve the health of the Aral environment. Even with efforts to improve the situation, the fate of the Aral Sea is irreversible. Uninformed decisions, made many years ago, have permanently scarred this land and its people. ■

We sometimes think we know more about nature than we do,
but there is a lot more to it that we don't understand.

Kofi Annan

Interesting Facts . . .

- Between 1965 and 1980 the amount of water entering the Aral Sea dropped from about 650 cubic yards (50 cubic kilometers) per year to zero.
- Contaminated dust from the Aral Sea has been found as far away as Pakistan and in the blood of penguins in the Antarctic.
- Aral Sea dust settling on glaciers in the Himalayas are causing them to melt at a faster-than-normal rate.

■ ■ ■ Three Gorges Dam—TAMING THE DRAGON

IN CHINA, people have been wrestling with a "river dragon" for thousands of years. The Yangtze. Turbid. Tempestuous. Legendary. Of all China's great rivers, it is the Yangtze that best symbolizes the history of a people blessed, and cursed, by the power of flowing waters. Known as the Golden Waterway, the Yangtze River brings water to 65 million acres (24 million hectares) of farmland, and prosperity to some 374 million people. For over 4,000 years, the emperors of China's "Middle Kingdom" made control of the Yangtze their chief preoccupation.

Yet, as late as the mid-twentieth century, those who lived, traveled, and worked on the Yangtze were still fearful of the fury this river could, and did, unleash. In 1954, one Yangtze flood left 30,000 people dead and 1 million homeless.

Citizens along its banks have no illusions about the destructive power of this river. But the power of this river is something that China wants desperately to harness.

As China's population continued to boom, energy needs grew. A project aimed at altering the flow, and fulfilling a dream of the ancient emperors, took shape.

Qutang, Wu, and Xiling are the Three Gorges of the mighty Yangtze. In 1984, hundreds of engineers, scientists, and technicians from all parts of China, and a dozen other countries, were drawn to this place of lore and legend. They planned not only to reshape the hills and valleys, but to tame the last dragon that resides here.

Today, humans move like ants across a massive, mechanized structure, one that will soon constitute the world's most powerful dam. Straddling the Yangtze for a distance of over 1 mile (2 kilometers), Three Gorges Dam will be 607 feet (185 meters) tall. Its enormous size will create a reservoir 372 miles (600 kilometers) long, with an incredible water storage capacity of 52 billion cubic yards (40 billion cubic meters).

Government projections show that by the time Three Gorges goes on line in 2009, its turbines will be able to generate almost 10 percent of China's electricity, replacing many air-polluting coal-fired power plants. Officials also point to Three Gorges' engineered ability to protect over 15 million people and 4 million acres (1.6 million hectares) of land along the Yangtze from devastating floods.

Yet, for all its stunning size, its stated promise, and its international backing, the Three Gorges Dam project is not without controversy. Current estimates of the great dam's final cost range from $25 billion to $65 billion dollars (£17 billion to £45 billion). Local and international organizations are concerned not only with Three Gorges' cost, but also with its impact on people and the environment.

In the race to completion, Three Gorges Dam will submerge tens of thousands of acres (hectares) from farmland and forest, 160 towns, 1,500 factories, and hundreds of archaeological sites. By completion, the project will have displaced over a million people. It will be the largest displacement in the history of dam construction.

Upstream, some 80 species of fish will be wiped out. Downstream, wetlands will be disrupted, and wildlife and fish populations endangered. Most ominous of all is the threat of catastrophic collapse. It is not an idle threat. In 1975, both the Banqiao and the Simantan dams failed, sending a surge of water downstream that killed over 200,000 people. It was a disaster that only became public years later.

These dangers appear so real that concerned environmentalists worldwide are advocating a halt to the Three Gorges Dam Project, opting instead for a series of five or six smaller dams placed strategically along the Yangtze. Such an alternative might avoid massive resettlement of people and provide a better match for energy needs with local areas of supply.

But despite alternative plans, despite growing uncertainty and opposition, construction continues on China's most ambitious project since the Great Wall. ■

We must treat each and every swamp, river basin, river and tributary, forest and field with the greatest care, for all these things are the elements of a very complex system that serves to preserve water reservoirs—and that represents the river of life.

Mikhail Gorbachev

Interesting Facts . . .

- In China, the Yangtze is called *Chang Jiang,* or "Long River." It is the world's third longest river, at 3,937 miles (6,300 kilometers).
- The dam's power output will be 18,200 megawatts, the equivalent to that of 18 nuclear power plants or burning 40 million tons of coal.
- Building the dam will require about 250,000 workers. Nearly 35.5 million cubic yards (27.2 million cubic meters) of concrete will be used.
- Some experts predict that pollution in the Yangtze will double as pollutants settle in the reservoir behind the dam. About 530 million tons of silt is expected to settle behind the dam each year.

The large corporations are suddenly getting a little bit frightened because suddenly the big thing is reputation management.

Anita Roddick

No one is perfect, you know, but you encourage industry to do more and more.

Ted Danson

The responsibilities of the private sector for the ecological consequences, as a result of their actions, are enormous indeed. That's why the private sector certainly can do a great deal to change the present situation for the better.

Mikhail Gorbachev

CHAPTER EIGHT

The Pipeline of Industry

IN VIRTUALLY EVERY CORNER of the globe, populations are growing, economies are developing, and industry is trying to keep up with an increasing demand for materials and products. In their efforts to meet this demand, industries face a critical dilemma: how to balance increased production goals while sustaining the natural resources that power industrial output.

Water is a key resource that is used by a spectrum of industries in a variety of ways. Industry is currently the second largest user of water worldwide, right behind agriculture. However, less than 10 percent of the water used by industry each day is incorporated into products. The remaining 90 percent is returned to its original source. But much of that water has been badly degraded, contaminated with by-products of mass processing.

The water fouled by industry poses a constant and long-lasting threat to all forms of life. Some of it seeps into aquifers. Some of it pollutes surface waters such as streams, rivers, and lakes, carrying toxins into coastal areas. And from the skies across many nations comes a new threat, acid precipitation—"black rain"—water recycled to earth, with residue from thousands of industrial smokestacks and other sources of toxic discharge.

Today, the toll may be measured in riverbanks choked with sludge, in the toxic tissues of fish, and in the health of many people who live near industrial sites. As we enter a new century, industry's debt to Mother Nature mounts.

■ ■ ■ Steel—USING WATER AS A COOLING AGENT

IN THE COMPETITION to design and manufacture better products, industrial alliances are as old as military alliances and quite often have been born of military necessity. For centuries, steel production has been an essential part of military victories, and the swords of Toledo, Spain, have became legendary for the quality of their steel.

Hammered from iron, tempered from steel, the Toledo blades have a history 2,000 years old. Warriors and nobles from as far away as Japan regularly journeyed to Toledo to observe an emerging steel tradition. They called it *Yaki-ire*, the hardening of steel by heating it to about 1,500 degrees Fahrenheit (800 degrees Centigrade), and then immersing it in water, abundant water, to ensure producing the finest blades in the world.

While water has always been used in steel production, the steel industry has often returned that water to the environment loaded with chemicals. From steel factories came greater and greater amounts of potent wastewater containing chromium, nickel, vanadium and molybdenum (used to manufacture steel alloys), and cyanide (used to pickle steel).

But a new way of thinking, of producing steel, is taking hold. One Japanese steel company is leading the industry in its environmental policies.

In modern-day Japan, "new" steels are leading the world into a new century of innovative products and applications. These steels are resistant to corrosion and thinner than paper, and they dampen vibration.

As a key agent for controlling the enormous amounts of heat that build up around the processing of molten steel, water is a necessity at this modern Japanese plant. But thanks to better process management, less water is now being used more effectively. In a plant that covers some 20 million square feet (6 million square meters) and turns out thousands of tons of product annually, the corporation's mission statement calls for increased production within an eco-friendly steel-making operation.

The company has reduced its water consumption from 150 to 135 tons of water per ton of steel. Here, water use in every stage of the plant is carefully designed for maximum efficiency, from the recycling of dust-collecting water in blast furnaces to closed-line water treatment in the hot rolling process.

The company is currently recycling 90 percent of its water back into the plant. The remaining water is filtered and treated before it is released into the environment.

Not only has the company been successful in keeping its environment clean, it has improved its position in the marketplace. Active promotion of its environmental policies has attracted a host of new customers who are also conscious of producing with eco-friendly raw materials. ■

To change what is happening to the environment, you have to involve government and you have to involve the private sector industry, because you cannot do it on your own. You don't have the money or the infrastructure, and they are the ones that are usually creating the problem—or we are, by needing what they make. So if they don't get involved, it won't work. So you need big business as an ally, you need industry as an ally.

Ted Danson

Interesting Facts . . .

- Between 1975 and 1998 the amount of energy needed to produce a ton of steel declined by 45 percent.
- Environmental controls add $10 to $20 (£7 to £14) per ton of steel to the manufacturing cost.
- Each year enough energy is saved by recycling steel to power 18 million households.
- In the last century, steel production has increased from 20 to 780 million tons annually.

■ ■ ■ Paper—USING WATER AS A PROCESSING MEDIUM

IN ANCIENT TIMES, water was as essential to industrial processes as it is today. Egyptian manufacturers of the pharaohs' time developed a process that used water to create a revolutionary new communication tool. In the burial wrappings of Egyptian mummies found near the modern city of Cairo, archaeologists have found papyrus, the oldest form of paper.

Papyrus was made from reeds growing in the water along the banks of the Nile. The outer coverings of the reeds were peeled away and the remaining stalks were cut into thin strips. Water was then used to soften the papyrus and activate the plant's natural bonding properties. Once softened, the reeds were layered, pressed, and dried.

This early water product was used primarily for parchment, or "old paper." It was the medium for works of literature, magic, religious texts, tax accounts, and correspondence throughout Egypt, Greece, and Rome. But while this "old paper" was a much valued and even rare commodity, attitudes toward "new paper" have often been another story entirely.

From office supplies to packing materials, from credit card slips to letter-quality bond, paper has become both a common and indispensable product the world over. Increased demand for paper has meant replacing small multiple-purpose mills with much larger specialty mills, some of which now use water to produce only pulp, the prime ingredient for paper. In some mills, it may take 91,000 gallons (350,000 liters) of water to make just 1 ton of paper.

But the most challenging environmental problem for modern paper mills has been to reduce the amount of polluted effluents they discharge into natural water systems.

The story of one extraordinary Canadian mill can inspire any industry. It places daily water management, conservation, and environmental safety on a par with profits. When this producer decided to build a state-of-the-art paper pulp mill at Meadow Lake, Saskatchewan, in western Canada, it faced a difficult situation. The area was blessed with high-quality aspen, access to electric power, good transportation, and a quality work force. But one piece of the puzzle was missing. The area's only available water source was the Beaver River. Celebrated for its clean water, the river had an extremely low flow, so low that in winter, the river froze altogether. Such a fragile water resource simply could not accept any effluents returned to it from a pulp factory.

This meant that the company had to design and implement a closed-loop water management system, a system that guaranteed zero effluents. It was something virtually unheard of for the paper industry, and for good reason.

Although new pulp and paper industry practices include recycling the water used in production, the degree to which water systems can be closed has always been limited by the contaminants that build up in the system during processing. When this mill's pulp was processed, it allowed chemical residues, including salts, to enter the wastewater from the mill at a rate of 440 pounds (200 kilograms) per ton of pulp. In order to recycle this wastewater, these complex residues first had to be removed.

The answer to this challenge came through applying a natural process to a high-tech setting—evaporation. Company engineers first collected every drop of wastewater. Solids were then removed by sedimentation and a technique called aeration/flotation. This clarified liquid was then evaporated to produce clean, distilled water, which could be recycled back into the milling processes. The result of this all-out effort was nothing short of amazing.

Unlike pulp mills of years past, this mill is able to use only 1 to 3 quarts (1 to 3 liters) of water per 1 pound (0.5 kilogram) of pulp. In addition, it is the world's first zero-effluent pulp mill. After ten years of operation, this record has remained intact. At a time when large-scale demand for product is increasing, this Saskatchewan-based mill is able to both conserve and restore water. In the process, it is keeping a legendary river pristine, despite being its major industrial neighbor. ■

Interesting Facts . . .

- It takes about 170 gallons (644 liters) of oil to produce 1 ton of pulp. The paper industry generates about 1,551 billion gallons (5,878 billion liters) of wastewater each year.
- About one third of the fiber used in pulp mills comes from recycled materials, with two thirds coming from virgin timber.
- In the South Bronx in New York City, a newsprint mill uses 3,800 gallons (14,400 liters) of water per ton of product. Eighty percent of it is recycled water from a sewage treatment plant.

■ ■ ■ Beer—USING WATER AS PART OF THE PRODUCT

WHILE SOME CORPORATIONS have redesigned their processes to preserve the environment, the battle is not over. Many industries in various parts of the world are still seeking to extract pure profit out of nature. Often, industries have lobbied successfully to block anti-pollution legislation. In other cases, those that could afford to pay fines for polluting have simply done so. Profits, they've reasoned, can offset any punitive damages. When this happens, where can water find a powerful champion?

Corporations have always tried to influence consumer choice, but it is a new development that consumer choice is influencing corporate behavior.

Informed consumers are making choices in a variety of industries, and the beverage industry is no exception.

Beer is an example of a product that is made from water, and for centuries brewers have known that it takes quality water to make quality beer. Many beer traditions have survived to this day. In Europe, medieval beer purity laws, the oldest food quality regulations known, still govern much of modern brewing.

Of the four ingredients for beer, water constitutes 92 percent of the beverage. The ancient process of brewing—changing water into beer—begins by carefully boiling water and grains until just the right moment. The master brewer knows exactly when the water has absorbed the right amount of the grain's flavor. Then a process of filtering and fermenting completes the transformation of water into this magical beverage.

In today's marketplace, the careful traditions of the master brewers must now be practiced on an industrial scale. First and foremost, a steady supply of quality water must be found. The very site of a brewery at the edge of Bangkok was determined by the presence of a 650-foot-deep (200-meter-deep) source of spring water. Recognizing its obligations to neighboring communities, this brewery has instituted high standards in all its uses of the local water supply. To guard against impurities and achieve the quality consistent with its brewing tradition, this brewery has instituted a scientific, water-quality-based approach.

We do really need to learn how to consume less. We need to develop technology that we can pass on to other developing countries. Because if they develop the way we did, it really will be a huge problem. If they develop the way we did, we really will sink the planet with pollution.

Ted Danson

Every beer is made with water that has first been analyzed for quality. This analysis can detect any pesticides from groundwater sources that have passed through agricultural areas. It can also detect any solvents, oil, or heavy metals that may have entered the water from another industrial source. The database from this analysis allows the brewery to act in time by extracting, treating, purifying, and softening the water that flows into its facility.

The quantity of water used in beer making is another issue of concern. While most breweries use up to 3 gallons (10 liters) of water for every 1 quart (1 liter) of beer produced, this brewery uses only 1.5 gallons (6 liters) of water for every 1 quart (1 liter) of beer.

Like many other industries, breweries must take into consideration possible harmful side effects to the environment from its waste. Each day, this brewery produces waste. And once this wastewater flows outside the brewery, it is collected in biodegradable treatment basins where it is purified, transforming it from a foaming brown liquid mass into crystal clear water again.

From the traditional to the modern brew masters, each successive generation of beer craftsmen has contributed to the battle for a clean environment. For not all breweries are using such high standards. It is only in planning and care that the purity of water can be preserved. Only through the purity of water can both the public and nature be served. ■

We have got to be penalized. We have got to stop endlessly whining about restrictions. If we mess things up, if we pollute, we should be penalized or we should be told we can't operate. It should be as strong as that.

Anita Roddick

Interesting Facts . . .

- Recipes for beer can be found on Babylonian tablets dating back to 4300 BC. Private beerhouses were maintained by both George Washington and Thomas Jefferson.
- In the middle ages beer was often safer to drink than water. This is also true today in some parts of the world.
- People in the Czech Republic consume about 42 gallons (160 liters) of beer per person, per year, the most in the world.
- Of all the beer sold in the U.S. almost 90 percent is "packaged beer," two-thirds in cans and one-third in bottles.

What is an environmental catastrophe or environmental disaster? It affects nature; it affects people; and not only our generation but also the generations that follow.

Mikhail Gorbachev

American Oceans Campaign wants to give a voice to the oceans. We want swimmable, fishable waters. One of the programs we are focusing on this year is a series of bills that would make it a law that every coast, every coastline, every beach in America would have to meet a certain water-quality standard—or be closed to the public. I think it is a very smart way to begin cleaning up coastal pollution.

Ted Danson

CHAPTER NINE

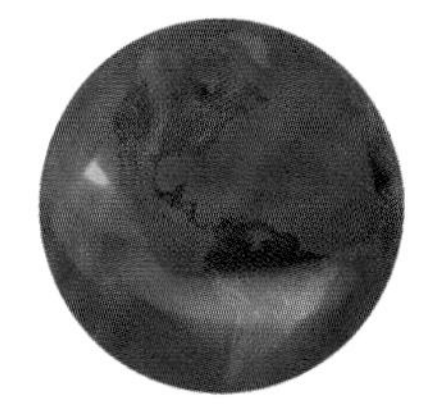

The Perils of Pollution

WATER TELLS US STORIES. Stories of its great journey—down from the sky, up from the earth, through homes, factories, and farms. More and more, the stories of water are tainted by pollution.

In their struggle to feed growing populations, farmers sometimes use fertilizers and pesticides. Agricultural pollution is a major problem in many areas, and it presents farmers with difficult questions about how to keep up with a growing demand for food, yet not pollute the environment. Some farmers understand the problem and only use chemicals when absolutely necessary, but as water passes through fields it picks up these elements and delivers them to rivers and aquifers. On an industrial scale, this presents a huge problem.

Industries are trying to keep pace with demands for more products and materials. On its passage through the world's factories, water collects a variety of toxins. If left untreated, this tainted water can wreak havoc in the environment.

And water travels through the homes and bodies of billions of people on the planet. If not properly handled, this wastewater further contaminates the global water supply.

Together these toxins are dramatically reducing our supply of clean, fresh water. Today, one billion people do not have access to safe drinking water. They also suffer a lack of sanitation that results in diseases that follow the paths of polluted waters across the land. Daily, 2 million tons of human excrement foul the rivers and groundwater of the world, creating widespread health problems and tragic deaths. Waterborne diseases are now the cause of nearly 15 million deaths each year.

KEELER BEACH
Fishing
Swiming, Surfing
Boating
CABANIAS For Rent
Safe Beach!
Fun!
Bait at Office
Prop: Norm Hoffman

■ ■ ■ London, 1854—A NEIGHBORHOOD PLAGUE

MUCH OF THE WORLD has yet to learn the painful lesson that Londoners learned over a hundred years ago about the link between water and disease. A cholera outbreak was spreading like a deadly wildfire through London and baffling local authorities. That is, until Dr. John Snow took a close look at the city's Broad Street neighborhood, where the highest concentration of cases was found.

The biggest project that the Carter Center has adopted for the last 12 years is the eradication of a horrible disease called "giddyworm," which comes from stagnant pools of water within which the giddyworm's eggs grow. And when a person drinks the water, a worm about 2 or 3 feet long grows inside their body, and through a very painful process emerges from their body.

Jimmy Carter

By mapping out the location of each cholera death, Dr. Snow was able to trace where that household fetched its water. He discovered that all victims had drawn their water from the Broad Street Pump, which may have been contaminated by sewage from a nearby house. In this case, the "cure" was simple. Dr. Snow had the pump handle removed. And by shutting off the supply of tainted water at its source, he stopped the epidemic from spreading further.

But cholera is only one of many diseases spread through polluted water, and cures are rarely so simple, especially if the condition is widespread or complex to treat. ■

In Milwaukee, people died because cryptosporidium, which came from animal feces, got into their water system. They turned on the tap water and drank it.
Ted Danson

Interesting Facts . . .

- In the Broad Street neighborhood epidemic 500 people died.
- London suffered two major cholera epidemics in the first half of the nineteenth century—one in 1832 causing 23,000 deaths and another in 1848 and 1849 causing 53,000 deaths.
- In the 1850s, Chicago began to pipe in water from Lake Michigan, reducing the reliance upon unsanitary wells and buckets of water from the sewage-filled Chicago River.
- Dr. John Snow was also a pioneer anesthesiologist. He helped introduce chloroform and ether anesthesia, and delivered two of Queen Victoria's children using chloroform anesthesia.

▪ ▪ ▪ Diarrhea—AN INTERNATIONAL PLAGUE

PERHAPS THE MOST DEADLY and widespread—yet most preventable—waterborne disease is diarrhea. It alone causes 4 million deaths each year. In many countries, the most common form of this disease comes from water contaminated by human waste. Infants afflicted with diarrhea can die in just a few days from the dehydration it causes.

In diarrhea clinics in Bangladesh, babies receive rehydration treatment that will give them a chance to fight the disease. But to effectively attack the problem, the source of pollution must be stopped. Since fighting disease-causing pollution can be long and costly, local communities often require the help of private Non-Government Organizations, or NGOs.

Among their hygiene and clean-water programs, local, national, and international groups in Bangladesh are actively promoting the construction and installation of good-quality, safe latrines. Local inhabitants are taking charge, mixing the cement that will form cylindrical containment walls. These concrete tubes become the foundation of quality latrines that prevent wastes from spreading into adjacent waterways.

As an added incentive, the program provides one free tube well for every group of ten families that can show they have installed latrines. But the installation of wells and latrines is only the beginning. The real hope for the future is education.

One example is a public park in Dhaka, capital city of Bangladesh. Actors from a national theater group educate while entertaining a large crowd gathered in the park. Using drama, humor, song, and dance, actors point out sources of polluted water and illustrate the growing threat to public health caused by this water. Through sponsorship from UNICEF and the NGO Forum for Drinking Water Supply and Sanitation, performances such as these help people see that by keeping daily water sources clean, they can dramatically reduce the spread of waterborne diseases.

But public theater alone will not reach and teach everyone. Recognizing the critical role women play in maintaining a healthy family, the NGOs have instituted workshops for women. Teachers travel to rural villages, presenting lessons in the fundamentals of good hygiene and effective sanitation.

A caseworker explains: "Some solutions are really very simple. For example, hand washing. We teach the community people and the school children to wash their hands properly with soap. But if they cannot afford soap, they can wash their hands using ash, because it is cheap, it is very much available, and it is really helpful to reduce the disease from their hands."

Overall, studies showed that national use of latrines in Bangladesh climbed from 4 to 35 percent throughout the 1990s. Hand washing after defecating rose from 5 to 27 percent. The use of well water for drinking climbed from 80 to 92 percent. While such small projects in local communities are beginning to have an effect, many more are needed. ■

Interesting Facts . . .

- The average adult suffers from diarrhea about four times per year.
- In Bangladesh only 39 percent of rural people and 41 percent of urban people have access to latrines.
- In the developing economies of Asia, 830 million people do not have access to safe drinking water, and 2 billion do not have access to safe sanitation facilities.
- To build a latrine costs about 11,880 Bangladesh takas ($220, £155). To install a tube well costs about 94,500 Bangladesh takas ($1,750, £1,238).

■ ■ ■ Moldova and Ukraine—A LETHAL LEGACY

IN MANY PARTS of the former Soviet Union, outdated industries have choked the waterways, unmonitored by crumbling bureaucracies and public service agencies. Ports on the Black Sea are heavy with the combined human and industrial pollution that threatens the health of the local population.

In the coal-mining village of Donetsk, years of unregulated industry have polluted the groundwater. Carbon dioxide, sulfur, zinc, and lead are just a few of the pollutants that have found their way into the water supply.

Adding to industrial pollution, disintegrating sewer systems are releasing human wastes directly into neighborhoods. People know they are living with a time bomb. With little money to rebuild infrastructure, residents' cries are falling on deaf and bankrupt ears.

In neighboring Moldova, poverty in the New Aneni region is so great that city dumps are frequented by scavengers seeking discarded treasures. These dumps add toxins to groundwater as rain filters through mountains of trash.

On local farms, decaying animal feces are seeping into the ground, and wells have become suspected sources of disease. In the face of such extreme poverty and dramatic infrastructure problems, local governments are powerless to address pollution issues.

Some municipalities have invited NGOs like Terra Nostra to assess their problems and to establish programs to monitor wells and test the water. They also build structures such as cement platforms for animal waste, to prevent it from seeping into the groundwater. Most importantly, they have convinced local residents not to wait for a bureaucratic bailout, but to begin action on their own. Vladimere Vygoing has heeded the call.

Now a local hero, he has spent the last several years volunteering his time and money to clean and reconstruct a seventy-year-old well. But it has been a daunting task for Vladimere: "We have emptied 20 tons of garbage from this well, and later on when we cover it with plates, I want to pave it with stones further to fill everything up with clay and to decorate everything and make it look decent. But of course we need assistance. The authorities pay attention, but we are just doing it by ourselves.

"It's hard, very hard. A sack of cement is expensive and here you need 1.5 tons. It's a lot of money. There is no money. It would be possible if we had the assistance to restore and dig springs, dozens or hundreds of them. So we are going to do it, but as long as we don't get assistance we do it by our own means. We do as we can."

It is people like Vladimere who are making a difference all over the world. Their individual efforts create a climate for action on a larger scale. ■

In some of the poorest nations on Earth where the water is filthy, the people are drinking it, and they get terrible diseases from it.

Jimmy Carter

Interesting Facts . . .

- During the Soviet era, military-related production accounted for more than 60 percent of Ukraine's industrial facilities.
- Ukraine has accumulated more than 100 million tons of toxic waste that need processing or safe storage.
- Almost 112 million cubic feet (3.2 million cubic meters) of raw sewage are dumped throughout Ukraine each year.
- Moldova receives more air pollution from surrounding countries that it produces nationally.

■ ■ ■ Father Rhine—THE REBIRTH OF A RIVER

THE RHINE RIVER stretches from its Alpine origins to a delta that empties into the North Sea. This water lifeline was once considered the most important and largest salmon river in Europe. But the hand of humans, and the effect of water pollution, changed all that.

Respectfully called "Father Rhine," and loved and trusted by the fishermen who relied on their river, it was painful to watch it grow ill, with prospects for recovery dimming every day. Heavy industry, manufacturing, and transportation all have gravitated to this very important international waterway.

By the 1970s, large quantities of untreated organic waste spawned a surge in the growth of bacteria in the river. Vast quantities of bacteria consumed the oxygen in the water and literally choked the river. In addition, toxic, non-degradable heavy metals began to accumulate in the remaining fish and river sediment, as mercury and cadmium pollution of Rhine sludge reached a peak. Aquatic fauna diminished considerably. Sensitive insects and fish died out.

To combat this acute contamination, the International Commission for the Protection of the Rhine (ICPR) mounted a number of projects. Major industrial plants, along with towns and communities, began discharging their effluents into wastewater treatment plants, instead of directly into the river. Many billions have been spent on cleaning wastewater.

The water quality of the Rhine has improved dramatically over the last thirty years. The percentage of oxygen in the water hit a low point in the early 1970s, and has been on the increase ever since. In the 1970s, most species of aquatic life had died out. Now there are almost as many species in the river as there were a hundred years ago.

Yet, even with the success of these cleanup and preventive measures, pollution might still flow into the Rhine. In November 1986, disaster struck. A fire broke out in Scheiserhalle. Extremely toxic chemicals went into the river, killing fish and animals as far downstream as the Lower Rhine, and impacting the daily life and finances of all those who depended on the river.

The Scheiserhalle disaster led to the institution of an ICPR surveillance system, focused on reacting quickly to accidents, as well as preventing them.

Currently, nine international monitoring stations, ranging from Reckingen in Switzerland to the three arms of the Rhine in the Netherlands, continually record water data. In addition, twenty national measuring stations monitor the Rhine and its tributaries. These surveillance stations work to identify main sources of pollution and determine whether antipollution measures are successful.

In order to respond quickly to such a disaster, the ICPR has installed computerized warning and alarm systems to alert all downstream communities, farmers, industries, and nations. By using these new systems, authorities can now quickly and accurately predict the journey of a wave of pollution in the Rhine, and its probable level of contamination.

A project called Salmon 2000 has been introduced into the improved waters of the Rhine. The project is aimed at helping salmon return from the seas and migrate up a portion of their former river habitat. The fact that it is working is significant, as one local fisherman declared: "The salmon say something about the quality of the water. It is a perfect fish for fishing and consumption. So when it exists in the river, the water is clean, and that's important."

With a vibrant ecosystem emerging, and water quality improving, the story of Father Rhine has taken an encouraging turn, and with proper care, the river will continue to heal itself. But success on the Rhine River is only one small victory in the battle to clean and maintain the world's water systems. ■

People should understand that, when dealing with nature, we have already exceeded the bounds of the permissible far too much. The situation is becoming dangerous. It affects people's health in a negative sense. If we go on treating nature the way we do now, we might find ourselves in a very difficult situation.

Mikhail Gorbachev

Interesting Facts . . .

- The Rhine river basin is the most industrialized region in the world, and the busiest waterway in the world.
- Between 1970 and 1985, nearly $38.5 billion (£27 billion) was spent in the construction of water treatment facilities along the Rhine.
- Agricultural runoff is now the major source of pollution in the Rhine.
- The International Commission for the Protection of the Rhine was founded in 1950, and remains active in its efforts to protect the river and its ecosystem against pollution and flooding.
- In 1993 several schools in France, Germany, and the Netherlands organized a cooperative environmental education project. The aim is to exchange various kinds of information about the local situation of the river among the participating schools.

I have traveled extensively and I have lived in many places, even in very modern places, modern cities where you cannot drink the water that comes from the faucet. Water is either delivered by trucks or you have to buy it in containers.

Isabel Allende

To me—someone who grew up in the Northern Caucasus, the region that suffered 52 cases of drought over a period of 100 years—water means a lot. There has always been a problem with freshwater supply in that area. I remember my childhood when I used to walk a distance of one-and-a-half kilometers to fetch some fresh water and bring it home. We also used to collect rainwater to do our laundry. In other words, shortage of freshwater has always been a pressing problem over there.

Mikhail Gorbachev

CHAPTER TEN

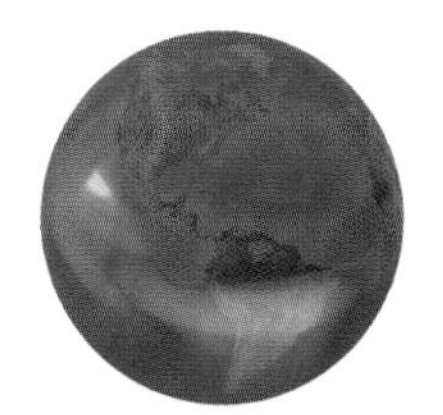

The Challenge of Transportation

ALL OF US NEED to transport water in some way or another. In many cities and towns, water travels to our homes from reservoirs through a large system of pipes and canals. Even if we live over a good source of groundwater, we still have to tap into the water with a pump and transport it through a small system of pipes to our faucets. But one out of every six people lack the simple convenience of a home faucet. They must hand-carry water daily from the well to their homes.

Getting water to homes and businesses is not such a simple task. For centuries we have been inventing ways to transport this vital resource. Some systems are inefficient and lose a great deal of water during transport. All systems require maintenance in order to keep the water flowing. Construction and maintenance involve money.

Transportation systems mix water with politics. Whoever is responsible for the construction, care, and maintenance of a water system usually has control over who gets how much, when, and at what price. Not everybody is happy with the decisions made regarding water transportation. The nature and politics of water transportation have an impact on a growing number of people and enterprises.

RJ·25
OASIS
98290 12345

■ ■ ■ The Masai—A WALK OF LIFE

AFRICA'S RIFT VALLEY stretches from central Kenya to Tanzania. It is a region of farmers, hunter-gatherers, and cattle herders. Here, the ritual of water transportation is at the very core of life for the pastoral people who roam the Rift, the Masai.

Masai women and children must embark daily on a walk for water—an activity that is literally a "walk of life." They gather in sisterhood at the water hole, where bonds are strong in times of peace and war.

These women, like others in similar regions the world over, congregate at rivers and streams, wells and wadis, to find and fetch water in a manner thousands of years old. Throughout the Rift Valley, where scarcity of permanent water sources combines with inadequate distribution systems, women and children of the Masai must shoulder the burden of transportation.

People in the villages all over the world know how precious water is. Especially the women, the women who go every day, sometimes twice a day, walking miles with a jar on their head to collect the water for the family, for cooking, for washing—for everything. They know how heavy it is, how precious it is, how much every drop counts.
Isabel Allende

Even a scant source of water is seen as nothing short of divine bounty. For, as every Masai knows, the gods may take the gift away without warning, leaving the land parched, its people and cattle hollow-eyed and helpless. Without this "walk of life," the Masai would have to abandon their nomadic ways and be forced to crowd around the few concentrations of natural water found in the Rift Valley.

From sources near and far, water must be transported daily in order to quench our thirst, feed our farmlands, fuel our industries, and process our wastes. Although many of us take this process for granted, even some world leaders understand this burden. ■

Women are the workhorses. Maybe five hours a day, just going to the well and gathering the water. The interesting thing about the well is, it becomes a center of communication. They tell stories around the well, they gossip about everything that's going on in the community. This happens around the world, so it becomes a social environment as well as just gathering the water.

Anita Roddick

Interesting Facts . . .

- The Rift Valley receives about 20 inches (500 millimeters) of rain annually.
- In a nomadic culture, an artificial well can be a problem in that it attracts people from outside the area, creating conflict for local resources. That competition for water forces women to walk farther for lesser-quality water.
- Water for a family of six weighs between 240 and 265 pounds (108 and 120 kilograms), which a woman usually carries on her head.
- The energy used in carrying water sometimes uses up one third of a woman's total daily calorie intake. This energy drain often results in anemia. Another major health problem associated with carrying water is skeletal damage.

■ ■ ■ The Aqueducts of Ancient Rome—A GRAND SYSTEM

TRANSPORTING WATER from the well to the home has always been a great challenge for people all over the world. Centuries ago, a practical solution was devised to move large quantities of water over great distances, using a simple, yet sophisticated, system designed to optimize the forces of nature. The aqueducts of ancient Rome proved to be one of the world's most notable water transportation systems.

We still marvel at the precision of the Roman architects whose aqueducts sloped only about 16 feet (5 meters) over a distance of 12 miles (20 kilometers). These impressive stone and concrete open channels used gravity to deliver a steady, unbroken water flow to the hearts of cities and towns within the Empire.

Water from aqueducts passed through an extensive distribution system—first into tanks to let the mud and pebbles settle, then by pipe into a tower called a castlellum. From there it flowed into several smaller tanks where lead or earthenware pipes would distribute it throughout the city.

Much water is being wasted by the wrong pipelines—it is being evaporated—many of them are old. We believe that 50 percent of the water is being wasted in the Middle East because of the inefficiency of the way water is being handled.

Shimon Peres

On average, it took seven years to build an aqueduct 20 miles (32 kilometers) long. Each aqueduct was named for the engineer in charge of the project, and each was known for the quality or flavor of its water. By 266 AD, eleven aqueducts channeled millions of gallons (liters) of water into Rome's 1,300 fountains and nearly 1,000 cold- and hot-water baths.

But despite their amazing functionality, the Roman aqueducts were not infallible. Upkeep was constant. Cement in the channels cracked, causing leaks. Limestone built up where water seeped and dripped, causing minerals to collect. And the use of lead pipes—which we now know causes serious toxic reactions and poses a tremendous removal issue—is thought by many to be an element of ill health that contributed to Rome's decline.

The problems that the Roman engineers faced are the same problems facing modern water transportation engineers—waste and improper handling during transport. ■

These problems are there for us to test ourselves, and to grow and to be clever and to use our brains.

Ted Danson

Interesting Facts . . .

- The Marcia aqueduct was famous for cool water while the Tepula aqueduct was know for warmer water.
- By 226 AD almost 300 million gallons (1,134 million liters) of water per day were delivered via the Roman aqueducts, 10 percent of which ran above ground.
- Water from the aqueducts was taxed by the size of the nozzle connection to one's home. Rome was plagued by water theft as people tapped into aqueducts and water pipes illegally.
- Rome had 144 public lavatories with streams of water running beneath them to carry away the waste.

■ ■ ■ The Central Arizona Project— GROWING CITIES IN THE DESERT

RISING OUT OF the Sonoran Desert of the American Southwest stands Phoenix, Arizona, a booming metroarea of commerce, residential neighborhoods, ranches, farms, and retirement communities. Lured from northern cities by the promise of sunny skies and economic opportunity, people have flocked to Arizona, raising the population by 80 percent since 1970.

The recent growth of Phoenix and other Arizona cities is indicative of the population shifts occurring in many regions of the world—toward arid climates where there is a greater demand for water—water that must be transported from distant sources. By the 1960s, overpumping of area aquifers had caused a steady drop in water tables. Earth fissures began appearing; the land near Phoenix and Tucson was settling. The city was using up more water than was available beneath Arizona sands. And the city was still growing. Water had to be imported on a large scale.

A partial solution to the problem came through a concerted effort by Arizona residents and the Federal Bureau of Reclamation to tap water from the once-wild Colorado River. Lake Havasu is the main holding tank of the Colorado River for the Central Arizona Project (C.A.P.). At Parker Dam, approximately 494 billion gallons (1,900 billion liters) of water are diverted from Lake Havasu toward Phoenix every year. All of that water is immediately lifted by huge pumps some 820 vertical feet (250 vertical meters) over a mountain at the rate of about 3,000 cubic feet (914 cubic meters) of water per second.

The water next enters a tunnel at Buckskin Mountain that is 7 miles (11 kilometers) long and 21 feet (6.5 meters) in diameter—large enough to drive a truck through. From there, it enters the Hayden-Rhodes Aqueduct, where it begins a journey of some 334 miles (538 kilometers) to the southeast.

People in the cities believe that they open a faucet and the water comes out like by magic.
They don't think of the effort—the incredible effort—to bring the water into the faucet.

Isabel Allende

Ironically, C.A.P.'s ultra-modern engineering could not be achieved without incorporating a familiar function from the ancient world. Borrowing from the Roman aqueducts, the Central Arizona Project employs gravity as a principle driving force for transporting river water. But in this case, the C.A.P. aqueduct is boosted every 14 miles (22.5 kilometers) by a series of pumping stations that lift the water back up again, moving gradually, steadily toward its final destinations in Phoenix and Tucson.

Part of the engineering marvel takes place just outside Phoenix. Here, a reversible channel allows water from C.A.P. to be pumped up and stored in Lake Pleasant during the winter months, typically a low-demand period. In the summer months, Lake Pleasant's water can be sent back along the reversible channel to meet the high demands of agriculture, homes, and businesses throughout the city.

Rains don't follow the customs,
rivers don't follow the frontiers,
and actually politics is limiting
the availability of water.

Shimon Peres

All of this activity is controlled by high-tech links to a central office, which constantly monitors the water flow and quality. To ensure smooth running and prevent leakages that can waste tremendous amounts of this precious resource, C.A.P. engineers have built into the system maintenance features that are monitored on a continual basis. Canals are screened to clear floating debris and keep the water clean. Algae-eating carp have been introduced into the system to clean the natural buildup of algae.

With the federal government steadily reducing subsidies for water development in the region, C.A.P.'s $4 billion (£2.8 billion) price tag is becoming a burden for Arizona consumers. But the real price of C.A.P. is far-reaching and has consequences for a much broader region politically, environmentally, and socially.

Whether or not we want to admit it, there is a high price to pay for moving water to turn deserts into cities, farmlands, and playgrounds. And it is the less powerful and less privileged who pay the most. The ultimate impact of C.A.P. on the environment and the people in bordering Mexico has yet to be assessed.

But one thing is certain. When water is transported from one place to another, someone is left high and dry. ■

The Colorado River between Arizona and California up in Northern Arizona—it's this roaring, huge river. By the time it makes its way down to the Gulf of Mexico, it's gone. Completely. We have used absolutely everything. And we use it to make rice paddies in Arizona. We have golf courses everywhere. I love golf courses. I don't mean to set myself apart, because I am part of this problem—absolutely. But we use it in the most extraordinary ways. We use it to turn deserts into places that have high humidity, that have lawns and palm trees.

Ted Danson

Interesting Facts . . .

- C.A.P. was originally designed for agricultural use only. Today, of C.A.P.'s 80 major customers 75 percent are municipal or industrial, 13 percent are agricultural districts, and 12 percent are Native American communities.
- C.A.P. was 40 years in planning and 15 years in construction.
- Diversion of the Colorado River began in the late 1800s, sending river water to California's Imperial Valley. In 1997, for the first time, the demand on the Colorado River exceeded the supply.

■ ■ ■ Water Bags—FROM TURKEY TO CYPRESS

IN A SEASIDE HARBOR on the Mediterranean, a unique experiment in water transportation techniques is bringing water to those in need. In 1997 Turkey signed a deal to bring millions of gallons (liters) of water to the island of Cypress. By boat.

Tugboats tow huge plastic bags filled with water from Turkey to Cypress. Each bag contains 32,800 cubic feet (10,000 cubic meters) of water. Magne Dale is captain of one of these Norwegian vessels, the *Orion*. He recalls the first water-bearing voyage. "Well, the first time we brought water over to Cyprus, we were received like heroes over there. They had no water. We were blowing the whistle, the President was there pressing the button, and the water came out. It was very nice. They were quite happy about it."

The joy was short-lived, however. Transportation systems mix water with politics, and in 1999 this water-towing vessel was barred from leaving port for weeks at a time due to political maneuverings by the Turkish government.

With any large transportation system, someone has a hand on the switch, and therefore has control over the item being delivered—in this case, water. And whenever there is control of a resource, money, power, and politics are involved.

It doesn't matter whether water is transported via a "walk of life," common well, canal, irrigation ditch, or the most high-tech pipeline. Wherever water is scarce, issues will arise—issues that involve ownership, borders, power, and money. These issues must be addressed, fairly, and with an eye to the future well-being of our neighbors and our environment, as we struggle to keep pace with growing demand. ■

Interesting Facts . . .

- An entrepreneur in California recently towed 770,000 gallons (2.9 million liters) of water in water bags from Humboldt Bay to the Golden Gate Bridge.
- Beginning in 1960, Cyprus began a program of building dams and reservoirs to collect the island's water. The slogan for the program was "No drop of water to the sea." In spite of this effort, severe drought since 1991 has caused acute water shortage on the island.
- Turkey has plans to build a $250 million (£177 million) pipeline under the sea to bring water to Cyprus.

A Tale of Two Farmers— SPAIN'S TAJO–SEGURA PROJECT

WITH AN ANNUAL RAINFALL of only 14 inches (350 millimeters), the southeast of Spain has a desert-like climate and landscape. In this arid environment, Jose Ferrer Sanchez runs a profitable citrus orchard. Sanchez is on the receiving end of the Tajo–Segura Water Supply Channel. Jose recalls life before water was imported to his region. "Before the pipes came it was all dry land without trees. Land with only some barley and plants that hardly grew. There was nothing."

When the Allies defeated the Axis powers in World War II, American GIs brought some of their culinary tastes to Europe. Soldiers loved iceberg lettuce on their cheeseburgers and, for awhile, planeloads of it arrived each week from California. When the Americans saw that the Murcia area of Spain was similar to California, they came up with the idea of encouraging the Spanish to grow their own iceberg lettuce. The only problem was water.

The Segura River could supply some water to the region, but not enough. The Tajo River could supply water to Murcia, but it was 250 miles (402 kilometers) away. Still, with the end of the war, and export potential apparent for agricultural product grown in Murcia, Spain decided to risk an investment in water transportation. In 1968, the Franco government built the Tajo–Segura Water Supply Channel. Today, water from the Tajo and Segura rivers is transported via huge channels, pipelines, and aqueducts to Murcia.

Twice monthly Jose Sanchez pays his water bill. This enables him to keep his private reservoir supplied with water that has traveled the remarkable journey from the Tajo River.

In Spain, as in Arizona, water is transported and stored in a system of huge canals, pipelines, and reservoirs. At the Talave Reservoir, the Tajo is joined by water from the Segura River. The Ojos Pumping Station catapults water straight up the side of a mountain at a rate of 72 cubic feet (22 cubic meters) of water per second. The LaPadera Reservoir is the last holding tank before the water reaches Murcia via the Mantaza aqueduct, a structure that is a direct descendant of Roman engineering.

The gift of water has brought life to farmlands in this region. So much life that Murcia is now called the "Kitchen Garden" of Europe. But some say that this gift of water is actually stolen property, pilfered from farms in one region and transported to fields in another.

Clemente Cervantes Crevelle's hands now pound the keys of a municipal typewriter, but this was not always the case. Low water levels in the Segura River, caused by a combination of drought and diversion of the waterway, forced Clemente to abandon his peach orchard in 1994. "The water has been diverted through Molina and to Orihuela, but it actually does not reach Orihuela. They are in even worse shape then we are. The Segura is almost dry."

Loss and gain, success and doom. One man's field of citrus, another's field of dust. The ingenious methods of diverting and transporting water to dry regions all over the world carry undeniable human consequences that often reach far beyond the original vision. Even in the most thoughtful of plans, unforeseen problems can arise. ■

Water in daily life [comes] through pipes, through taps; apparently as if it's something limitless. That's not the case. There is limitation. On one hand, our whole life depends on water and that very thing is limited. So we have the responsibility to take care about water.

The Dalai Lama

Interesting Facts . . .

- The average price for production of water in Spain is 229 pesetas ($1.19, £0.8) per cubic meter.
- In Spain, 17 percent of the cost of water is for purification, 49 percent is for distribution, and 34 percent is for waste treatment.
- Most of Spain receives less than 24 inches (600 millimeters) of rain annually.
- A single golf course consumes as much water as an entire town of 10,000 people.

We're going to be having lots of negotiations and conflicts between states where one of the major issues would be water, and who controls the source.

Kofi Annan

I can see solutions: The moment that the parties (all nations) will agree to see nature as the overriding consideration—more than politics. Politics divides people, wastes energy, wastes money, wastes time. If the countries will agree to handle water as it flows by nature, all of us will win, without exception.

Shimon Peres

CHAPTER ELEVEN

Water—War and Peace

DOES ANYBODY OWN WATER? Perhaps not, but there are people who control water. Many rivers throughout the world cross borders. Borders of property lines, borders of states, of provinces, and borders of nations. Controlling the natural flow of a river, in many cases, means controlling the precious resource of a neighbor or a nation.

This means people upstream can deny life-giving resources to people downstream. If this happens, people on the downstream end are surely not going to sit still while their water flow is halted. But what happens when only some of the water is diverted upstream? How much is too much? Who has the authority to make the decision? With the importance of clean, fresh water dramatically increasing, it is no wonder that many experts claim that the next wars will be fought over water.

Control over water offers great potential for conflict, but it also offers opportunity for dialogue. With dialogue comes interaction, and interaction opens the door for understanding. We are reaching a point in time on our planet when we will have to choose between conversation and combat over this life-sustaining liquid.

■ ■ ■ Water Court of Valencia— JUSTICE FOR FARMERS, DECIDED BY FARMERS

VALENCIA, SPAIN, famed for its farm produce, is also home to a time-honored ritual of justice. It is called *El Tribunal de las Aguas*, "The Water Court." Since the tenth century this court has been meeting weekly outside the Cathedral of Valencia.

Every Thursday at noon a procession of judges assembles to provide an informal, but fully respected, forum for farmers to settle water disputes. The court's jurisdiction is limited and its forms and procedures are unconventional, but every farmer in the region takes it seriously, because the court keeps water violations in check, and prevents conflicts from growing.

All of these issues are still being studied—not yet completely understood—and in the future will be debated. And they might very well involve lawsuits; they might very well lead to war.

Jimmy Carter

The judges in this court are not legal professionals, but *hombres del campo,* "men of the soil," elected by fellow farmers, and there are no lawyers. Not only is this court free, but decisions are handed down immediately after evidence has been presented.

Courts such as *El Tribunal de las Aguas,* run by the people and for the people, present an effective way to handle water conflicts on a local scale. On an international scale, however, the issues are far more complex, and the methods for resolving them, far more challenging. ■

War over water would be an ultimate obscenity.
And yet, unfortunately it is conceivable.

Queen Noor of Jordan

Interesting Facts . . .

- From 1094 until 1099, Valencia was ruled by the Spanish hero El-Cid.
- The cathedral, outside which the water court assembles, used to be a mosque, and was converted when James I conquered Valencia. Construction of the building took 150 years.
- Spain has recently imposed a new law mandating the metering of water for agriculture.
- Common law practices in the United States employ the "riparian doctrine," which views the watershed as an integral natural unit.

■ ■ ■ Great Anatolia Project—A TURKISH DILEMMA

THE POWER PLAYS over two great rivers in the Middle East have been heating up in a three-pronged struggle—among Turkey, Syria, and Iraq.

Turkey is harnessing the Tigris and Euphrates rivers with a series of dams in a grand irrigation and hydroelectric plan. The plan, known as the Great Anatolia Project (G.A.P.) has clear benefits for Turkey.

Scheduled to be complete in 2005, the G.A.P. project will irrigate 4.2 million acres (1.7 million hectares) of land. The increased agricultural output, along with the increased power provided by the project, will help Turkey develop as a nation, both economically and socially. For a country whose population is expected to rise to 25 million by 2010, Turkey's long-term plan for controlling the flow of these rivers is highly desirable.

The future now looks brighter for people like Emine Getinas, a young Turkish professional. "Something beautiful is happening; there is a new life for me. For my generation, they haven't done anything in this area. The younger people have emigrated to find a job, but through this dam we get new houses, new gardens that will be built for us. A lot of jobs will be created. I have confidence; the young have confidence."

But Turkey's G.A.P. project is the cause of deep concern to its downstream neighbors, Syria and Iraq. Like Turkey, Syria is also a rapidly developing nation. Syria's plans for economic growth include using Euphrates River water for irrigation of its northern territories. To provide for this growth, Syria's Taqba Dam and other Syrian dams on the Euphrates were designed with the potential to irrigate 1.6 million acres (640,000 hectares) of land.

But Syria contends that Turkey's G.A.P. project has inhibited this potential by reducing the water flow downstream and steadily undercutting the power of the Taqba Dam. The Syrian government estimates that once Turkey's G.A.P. project is completed, the flow of Euphrates water to Syria will be reduced by a drastic 40 percent.

Meanwhile, Iraq contends that the G.A.P. project will reduce *its* water flow by a still-more-damaging 90 percent. With Turkey's control of water at the heart of this conflict, sites of the Great Anatolia Project have become potential terrorist targets that must be heavily guarded.

In the growing conflict over water rights, Syria is supplying both arms and operational land bases to the PKK, Turkey's Kurdish separatists. And in an unprecedented alliance, Syria has sided with its traditional rival, Iraq, to both condemn and undermine Turkish water dominance.

Saber rattling among these three countries over water rights may seem inevitable. Yet, the threat of war along the Euphrates River is not caused by a critical shortage of water. The water is there, and potentially available to all. So in an attempt to defuse growing tensions, Turkey has undertaken yet another plan, known as the "Peace Pipeline." This plan would divert water from Turkey's Senhan and Ceyhan rivers, and is projected to deliver an estimated 2,860 million cubic yards (2,200 million cubic meters) of water annually to Turkey's southern neighbors. But the "Peace Pipeline" has not yet realized its potential, and Syria and Iraq doubt that it ever will.

As the need for more food and greater economic development heightens along the Tigris and Euphrates, tensions mount and the danger of a war over water threatens. ■

Water has been a source over so many years of erosion of confidence, of tension, of human rights abuses, really, of so many in areas whose traditional water supplies have been controlled and depleted by occupational authorities. That must stop if we're going to be able to develop a climate for peace.

Queen Noor of Jordan

Interesting Facts . . .

- The dams along the Tigris and Euphrates supply almost 50 percent of Turkey's electricity.
- In Turkey, 10 percent of the population owns 75 percent of the land.
- The Euphrates provides Syria with about 85 percent of its water.
- Four times the annual flow of the Euphrates River can be stored in the reservoir behind the Ataturk Dam.

■ ■ ■ Draining Paradise—THE OKAVANGO RIVER DISPUTE

THE OKAVANGO RIVER is a water lifeline running through southern Africa. Rising out of the Benguela plateau of Angola, the Okavango dallies briefly in Namibia's Caprivi Strip before rolling on into Botswana and large stretches of the Kalahari Desert.

One river, three nations—each voicing its own notions about how to allocate the water. It's a recipe for conflict. In 1994, Namibia, Botswana, and Angola recognized that to effectively combat both drought and conflict, they would have to find a way to share their scarce resource.

All was well until 1996, when Namibia proposed to construct a water pipeline 620 miles (1,000 kilometers) long. The objective: to pump up to 26 million cubic yards (20 million cubic meters) of water annually from the Okavango River to Namibia's rapidly growing central area, including its capital city of Windhoek.

While the pipeline would fulfill Namibia's need for more water, Botswana is concerned about its effect on river water that now creates a natural paradise, the Okavango Delta, where over 100,000 people live.

Olive Sephuma, a Botswanan environmentalist, expresses her concern. "Many communities live in and around the Delta. These same communities are concerned that if Namibia's pipeline plan goes ahead, there will be less water coming through to them and their lives will be changed irrevocably.

"We think that the Namibian government should look at other alternatives before considering a plan that puts so many lives and the wildlife and the tourism industry at stake, and might very well dry up the Delta forever."

Known as the Jewel of the Kalahari, the Okavango Delta is both an environmental gem and Botswana's prime tourist attraction. Here, the waters of the Okavango River turn the "great thirst land" of the Kalahari into one of the world's largest inland wetlands. This delta is a haven for numerous species of wildlife. But droughts have already dried up much of the southern part of the delta.

As I travel around the world, people think the only place where there is potential conflict [over] water is the Middle East, but they are completely wrong. We have the problem all over the world.

Kofi Annan

In an attempt to resolve this complicated issue peacefully, a joint water management commission has been established, representing all three nations. The commission will carefully evaluate the effects of a Namibian water pipeline on the downstream flow of the Okavango River and will consider all arguments. But finding acceptable solutions to this multi-national "environment-versus-development" conflict is an extremely difficult task, further complicated by the knowledge that droughts will inevitably return to this parched region of Africa.

Peacekeeping plans to solve water disputes will have to be in place before the droughts return. Otherwise, as we have seen in other parts of the world, conflicts between water-stressed peoples may lead to desperate actions. ■

The negotiation process is one that really only will succeed when there is a recognition that the equitable distribution of resources—the most vital of all, of course, water—is the only guarantee that any states will have of stability and peace and security in the future.

Queen Noor of Jordan

Interesting Facts . . .

- In 1996 Namibia managed to reduce its water consumption to 1989 levels even with a 35 percent increase in population. The demand for water is expected to double by 2020.
- Tourism in the Okavango Delta is a $250 million (£178 millon) per year industry.
- The Okavango Delta is home to 164 species of mammals, 540 species of birds, 157 different reptiles, 80 species of fish, and thousands of varieties of insects.
- In Botswana there are three times more cattle than people.

■ ■ ■ On the Edge of Crisis—THE ARAB-ISRAELI CONFLICT

FOR THE PAST HALF-CENTURY, the Jordan River has been a key to the growth of the modern nation of Israel. But it has also become the source of life and hope for *all* people in this region.

Ending its journey in the Dead Sea, the Jordan River begins some 200 miles (322 kilometers) to the north in a mountainous region on the borders of three nations. About 6 miles (9.6 kilometers) below the Sea of Galilee, the Jordan River is joined by waters from the Yarmuk River. The Yarmuk, whose major sources are in Syria, forms the border between that country and the nation of Jordan.

Modern-day conflicts over both Yarmuk and Jordan river waters began in the 1950s, when the state of Israel began to take shape. To "make the desert bloom," Israel needed water from both the Jordan and the Yarmuk. From 1953 to 1964, Israel built the National Water Carrier, a complex of canals, pipelines, and tunnels designed to transport water from the Sea of Galilee region to the coastal plain of Israel and the Negev Desert.

But other nations needed that water too. Many Arabs feared that Israel's National Water Carrier would divert far too much Jordan River water south of the Sea of Galilee. This, they reasoned, would pose a threat to downstream neighbors, Jordan and Syria. In 1964, the First Arab Summit proposed to stifle Israeli plans. The following year, Syria began construction of the Headwaters Diversion Plan, whose goal was to prevent Jordan River water from reaching Israel.

In the summer of 1965, the Israeli military responded with an open attack on the Plan's construction sites. Major General Israel Tal remembers Israel's response. "We knocked out the Syrian earth-moving equipment and other kinds of equipment by tank gunfire. Then we attacked with the air force... They had to give up, and the project of the diversion of the sources of the Jordan River and depriving Israel of its water was terminated."

Two years later, as a result of the Six-Day War, Israeli forces conquered parts of Egypt, Syria, and Jordan. By gaining control of Syria's Golan Heights, the Israelis held two of the three headwaters of the Jordan River. They also seized the West Bank of the Jordan, the Gaza Strip, and the Yarkon-Taninim Aquifer, which currently supplies one-third of Israel's freshwater supply.

As a consequence the imbalance between the nations is dramatic, with Israel having eight times the water resources of the two, and a quarter-million Palestinians living in the West Bank and the Gaza Strip.

While droughts drag on summer after summer, Palestinian villages have water only one or two days each week. Often, villagers must buy their water from private vendors at high prices. Tensions are inflamed in areas like the Gaza Strip by Israeli settlers who receive water by being hooked into the national water supply. Frustration is high as both sides live with the threat of conflict.

As Nir Peleg, an Israeli settler, put it, "In my opinion the water situation will not get any better. Not for the Jews, neither for the Palestinians. The situation is only getting worse and I think that the Jews at least will have to find the solution in finding other provisions."

Palestinian farmers in the Gaza Strip also suffer from lack of good water. Each year the groundwater level drops 6 to 8 inches (15 to 20 centimeters). As a result, saltwater now intrudes several miles (kilometers) inland from the Mediterranean Sea, spoiling crops that cannot be salvaged.

The "haves" and the "have nots" are clearly divided here, and for years, it seemed this would continue to be the source of water disputes in the Middle East. But the 1994 peace treaty signed by Israel and Jordan offered a glimmer of hope. Ideally, the achievements of the Israeli–Jordanian Peace Treaty will serve as a model for the resolution of other hydrological disputes in the region. ■

Interesting Facts . . .

- Annual rainfall varies in Israel from 40 inches (1,016 milimeters) in the north to 1.25 inches (31.75 milimeters) in the south. Nearly 60 percent is lost to evaporation.
- In the Gaza Strip the nearly 1 million Palestinians use 25 percent of the available local groundwater, while the 3,000-4,000 Israeli settlers use the remaining 75 percent.
- The West Bank Mountain Aquifer currently supplies Israel with one-third of its water, and is one of Israel's main concerns in ongoing peace negotiations.
- The Middle East holds 0.9 percent of the world's water supply and 5 percent of the world's population.

Water is one of the many aspects in which we have to struggle for life—and we have been doing it—and we will eventually restore that balance that is so necessary right now.

Isabel Allende

We've just taken it for granted for so long. And it is not bad to have to wake up. It is not bad to have these problems. We just have to wake up and deal with them. It's not doom and gloom. It's not the end of the world. It's all fixable. But we have to wake up and not pretend that there isn't a problem.

Ted Danson

CHAPTER TWELVE

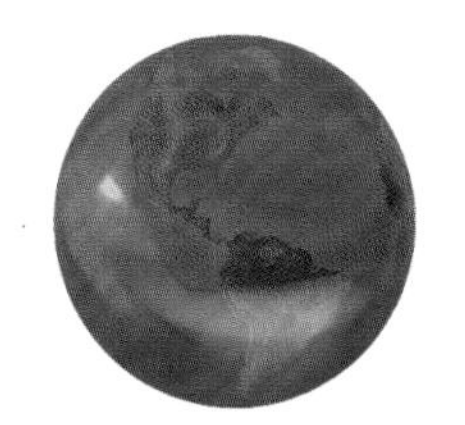

Facing the Future

WITH THE BEGINNING of the twenty-first century, humanity will soon enter an unprecedented era of challenge. For millions of people, worldwide, the well is literally running dry. We must change both our attitudes and our practices in order to sustain the well.

Fortunately, there is hope. All over the world people are experimenting with new ideas and new technologies. Some of these are expensive high-tech solutions, while others are remarkably low-tech, practical alternatives. But technology alone is not the answer.

At the recent World Water Conference in The Netherlands, the single most important goal that came out of the conference was education. It is imperative that we create awareness of the difficulties that lie ahead and of the finite nature of this precious resource.

Water resources are unevenly distributed throughout the world, yet all over the world people must begin to see the horizon of need. Our neighbors' problems will soon spread to our backyards. Our future cannot exist without a better understanding of water, the drop of life.

■ ■ ■ Sana'a—RUNNING ON EMPTY

THE SANA'A REGION of Yemen is perched above the vast deserts of "the Empty Quarter" at the base of the Arabian Peninsula. It is here, legend tells us, that Shem, son of Noah, built the first city to emerge from the Great Flood, a dusty jewel on the shore of ancient seas. Despite its mythic stature, Sana'a is now a city wrestling with growing demands and pressing needs. The biggest of these needs is water.

For thousands of years, Yemen enjoyed abundant water. Its people gave daily thanks to Allah for the rains and rivers. Visit the *souks*, the marketplaces of Sana'a, and you will know something of water's vital role in this land of sand and mystery. Traditionally, Yemen's agriculture has supplied food for international trade as well as for domestic needs. But the colors fade and the sounds ring hollow in the face of a recent World Bank report: Yemen is running out of water.

We realize the total supply of water has not materially changed. And the demand for water has increased tremendously. And now the water that used to flow into the ocean, fades away to nothing before it ever reaches the ocean because everybody has used up all the water.

Jimmy Carter

All over the country, demands placed upon water supplies by Yemen's growing population are rapidly drying up old wells. Yemen's groundwater tables are sinking lower and lower. In Sana'a, the pumping of groundwater has resulted in almost complete depletion of an ancient resource, forcing many residents to dig wells as deep as 5,000 feet (1,524 meters). Many people must pay exorbitant prices for potable water obtained from private vendors. Or they tap from illegal sources.

If demand continues to rise, and local water resources remain the same, the Sana'a region will literally dry out by the year 2004. In an emergency effort, the government of Yemen has joined forces with the World Bank to implement water management projects that address this growing problem.

The country's entire water infrastructure is being reevaluated. New water treatment plants are under construction. The media is being recruited to spread the critical message of conservation. For Sana'a these actions may be too little, too late. Only time will tell.

Yemen is an example of a possible future for many humans on Earth. We now have to make choices if we are to survive on this planet. None of us can afford to take supplies of fresh water for granted any longer. ■

But these things you cannot achieve through prayer but through effort. Through vision and through a wider perspective view. That's the only way.

The Dalai Lama

Interesting Facts . . .

- Inhabited for 2,500 years, Sana'a is possibly the oldest continuously inhabited city.
- Ninety percent of the population of Yemen live on 3,150 cubic feet (90 cubic meters) of water per year.
- Sana'a has been pumping groundwater at a rate 4 times faster than the aquifers are recharged by nature.
- About 22 percent of Sana'a's water is used for growing qat, a mild narcotic. The young leaves of this plant are chewed by a majority of the men of Sana'a.

▪▪▪ Los Angeles—ILLUSION OF ABUNDANCE

CITIES LIKE LOS ANGELES, California, are facing some of the same challenges as Sana'a. The population of Los Angeles is expected to grow 20 percent by 2015. That means a 20-percent increase in the demand for water in a city that is already being forced to look for new sources of water.

Since the Ice Age, Mono Lake has been fed by creeks and streams, each flowing from the nearby Sierras, each acting in concert to reduce the lake's level of salinity. As a result, this unique water resource northeast of Los Angeles developed an early and unique ecosystem.

Possessing no outlet, Mono Lake is a habitat for brine shrimp and brine flies. Millions of ducks used the lake and surrounding bottomlands for refueling during migration. California gulls arrived here annually to breed and to nest. Fish thrived in the lake's tributaries. Exotic birds, including pharlaropes, eared grebes, yellow-bellied marmots, and long-billed avocets, visited Mono Lake before their non-stop flights to South America.

But starting in 1941, human intervention began to take a dangerous toll on this realm of birds, brine shrimp, and gothic landscape. In an effort to capitalize on its cheap source of drinking water for a growing population, the Los Angeles Department of Water and Power began diverting the water that flowed into Mono Lake, sending it through a man-made river, straight to the city.

Over the next twenty years, the results were catastrophic. Without its constant fresh water infusion, Mono Lake's water level began to drop dramatically—18 inches (46 centimeters) each year—as 17 percent of L.A.'s total water supply was diverted from Mono Lake's feeder streams. Islands, which were important nesting sites, suddenly became peninsulas, each one vulnerable to predators. Stream ecosystems disintegrated due to lack of water. The trout population of local streams all but disappeared. And air quality deteriorated as the exposed lakebed became a source of airborne particles, which violated the Clean Air Act. Something, or someone, had to save Mono Lake from the ravages of stream and creek diversion.

In September 1979, a group of 20,000 concerned citizens, called the "Bucket Walkers," filled containers with water in Los Angeles, trudged nearly 300 miles (483 kilometers) to the Great Basin, and poured the stolen water into Mono Lake. It was a gesture of defiance that hit home with conservationists.

Perhaps water shortage will be a really good thing for this country. I think that when you start running out of water you'll start to get smart. You start to develop technology that saves it, that cleans it, that re-uses it, and in essence you won't be dumping so much of it into the ocean, carrying all of our toxins with it.

Ted Danson

The city's neighboring power block, the San Joachin Valley farmers, did not wish to pay anything extra for water to nurture its crops. As a result, they supported L.A. in its continued diversion of Mono Lake feeder water. This power block posed a significant threat to conservationists throughout the state. It would be a twenty-year struggle, waged in David-and-Goliath fashion through court after court.

In 1983, citing the Mono Lake diversion as a public trust violation, the California Supreme Court ruled that no water can be taken from a stream, river, lake, or other natural source without a careful assessment of the harm it might do. For the first time, the courts were stating their responsibility for assessing the dangers to the environment from water diversion.

In 1994 a court order was issued to reduce the amount of water the city was importing from the rivers that fed Mono Lake. In order for Los Angeles to meet increased demand with shrinking supplies, the city has stepped up its conservation and recycling efforts. A program to distribute free, low-flush toilets has reached more than 700,000 homes. Recycling programs are sending reclaimed water to parks and gardens all over the city.

Through combined low- and high-tech efforts the city hopes to use 10 percent less water by the year 2010 despite a growing population. This is not a certain future, however, and the city is still struggling to raise awareness of the importance of water conservation among its citizens. ■

Interesting Facts . . .

- Since 1970 only 15 percent of L.A.'s water supply has been pumped from local wells.
- Fixing a leaky faucet saves 20 gallons (75.8 liters) of water per day.
- Collecting water for gardening from the faucet while waiting for hot water to warm up saves about 250 gallons (947 liters) per month.
- Using a broom to clean the sidewalk instead of a hose saves 150 gallons (568.5 liters) of water.
- Using a pool cover prevents about 1,000 gallons (3,790 liters) per month from evaporating.

■ ■ ■ NASA—WATER OUT OF THIS WORLD

IN OUR QUEST for survival, humans have always sought new frontiers. In exploring these frontiers, we have gained knowledge that has revealed new possibilities for the future. Since the 1960s, space missions have shared one thing in common: the challenge of using and reusing water. Water cannot be compressed, and has always been a heavy, bulky element to carry into space.

At the Johnson Space Flight Center in Houston, Texas, new technologies are being developed that may one day help us preserve water, both in space and on Earth.

Albert Bahrend of NASA's Advanced Life Support Systems lab explains the need. "We are really cutting the umbilical cord with Earth when we go off on these long-duration missions, like a 1,000-day mission to

We have the knowledge, the resources, the technology, and the will. I'm sure that this is something that will be the first priority in the next hundred years. And we will be able to solve it. I have great faith in our capacity as human beings to destroy and to construct. I don't think that we will destroy ourselves on the planet, I'm an optimist. I believe that we will survive and we will prevail.

Isabel Allende

Mars. You cannot take everything with you that you really need. So you take a bare minimum and you recycle that as you progress through the mission."

In a high-tech lab, efficient and compact systems are being developed to recycle all the water that is used in a space mission. This includes water from laundry and showers, even urine. In a closed chamber at the Johnson Space Center, Astronaut Karen Meyers was part of a crew that was testing NASA recycling systems. "I spent sixty days living inside a closed chamber. The primary reason for these kinds of tests is to take recycling hardware, place it inside a chamber, and then provide real-life waste streams coming from human beings."

If these machines are going to keep astronauts alive while they are living and working in space, we have to make sure they are functioning as fully integrated systems.

The systems must not only clean the water but also the systems themselves. Harmful bacteria can build up in hoses and valves and can subvert the recycling process.

On extended missions, water will be needed to grow food, and NASA is also experimenting with ways to increase yields with minute amounts of water.

And NASA has found water on the moon, on Mars, and even on asteroids. This offers hope for collecting water on deep-space exploration missions.

As often happens in exploring new horizons, we gain new perspectives on our old problems. As Karen explains, the astronauts value the view from space. "The astronauts tend to spend a lot of time looking out the window at that beautiful blue planet. That is really their touchstone, in all the time they spend revolving around it." ■

We must treat water as if it were the most precious thing in the world, the most valuable natural resource. Be economical with water! Don't waste it! We still have time to do something about this problem before it is too late.

Mikhail Gorbachev

Interesting Facts . . .

- NASA conserves weight for flights by separating water from food. Food is then rehydrated as astronauts prepare meals.
- The spaces shuttle's fuel cells combine hydrogen and oxygen to make electricity. This also produces water.
- Aboard Skylab a collapsible cylindrical shower collected water as it was being used for cleaning.
- There is evidence of floods on Mars.
- NASA has found ice on the moon which is thought to have been brought there by meteorites.

■ ■ ■ Desalination—TAKING THE SALT OUT OF THE SEA

LOOKING BACK AT EARTH from space we can see a vast source of water that may help relieve our terrestrial water problems. For long-lasting answers to the global water crisis, scientists are now looking to the very place where primordial life began, the sea. Today, the earth's surface is 70 percent water, and 97 percent of that water is saltwater.

"Water, water everywhere...but not a drop to drink." So goes "The Rime of the Ancient Mariner." Since ancient times, we have wrestled with the question, What if we could transform saltwater into fresh clean drinking water? Think of the possibilities! The Greeks thought of the possibilities. In the fourth century BC, Aristotle wrote, "Saltwater, when it turns into vapor, becomes sweet... and the vapor does not form saltwater again when it condenses."

The Romans thought of the possibilities. In 49 BC, Julius Caesar's legions experimented successfully with solar distillation, converting seawater, on a small scale, to drinking water. By the mid-nineteenth century, the British and American navies were using a handful of desalination devices onboard ships.

And when we say that we would like to have a better world, a more beautiful world, one of the best partners is clearly water. We can—with water—better the world.
Shimon Peres

But today, the process of desalination still produces only one-quarter of one percent of mankind's daily fresh water needs. There are now nearly 11,000 desalination plants in the world, and 60 percent of those plants are in the Middle East. Saudi Arabia is currently the world leader in desalination, producing 30 percent of Earth's entire volume of distillate water. Today, distilled seawater accounts for 70 percent of the kingdom's potable water, an essential ingredient in Saudi agriculture.

For years, the cost of large-scale desalination has been affordable only to nations with enough oil surpluses to power their desalination plants. But technology is now bringing down the cost.

With arid and semi-arid regions possessing lots of sunshine, solar power may provide an answer to the cost of desalination.

Reverse osmosis is also a promising method. Through this process of desalination, pressure is applied to saltwater to force it through a membrane. Only pure water passes through, leaving the salt behind. Reverse osmosis costs about $2 (£1.4) per 988 gallons (3,800 liters).

With desalination plants all over the world producing fifteen times as much fresh water as they did in the late 1970s, our oceans continue to take on greater importance as a future source of our daily fresh water. ■

We do have to stop and plan. And we are capable of doing it, we certainly can. And there are little areas, here and there, that had great victories. You know, we can do it if we stop and plan and think of us as all in this together, and not us against them or I need to make mine, I need to get mine. We need to start thinking as a group, how to save this resource.

Ted Danson

Interesting Facts . . .

- When sea water freezes the ice crystals that form are without salt.
- In Saudi Arabia, the capital city Riyadh receives desalinated water transported over 300 miles (483 kilometers) from the gulf.
- The time needed for planning and constructing a desalination plant is 5 years.
- In various parts of the world over the next 5 years about $10 billion (£7 billion) worth of desalination plants will come on-line.

■ ■ ■ DRiWATER®—PLANTING A FOREST IN THE DESERT

FOR EGYPT, the future means finding ways to feed a rapidly growing population. This includes being able to farm in two unlikely locations, the Sinai and Sahara deserts. Building large-scale irrigation infrastructure is impractical in these remote desert regions. Yet across large stretches of barren terrain, an effort is underway to transform the desert into a fruitful oasis using a new technology called DRiWATER®.

DRiWATER® is a water-holding gel compound. Because the water is encased in the gel, it does not evaporate in the desert sun. Instead, the water is slowly released into the ground as the gel is eaten away by microbes in the soil. In a world grown wary of the effects of pollution, DRiWATER® is completely biologically degradable and free of chemicals that might poison the plants or contaminate the soil.

Putting all these things together, you can learn from each other, which is one important thing. Altogether we can make the system work. Use a little from everything.

Johan Cruyff

"Drip irrigation in a box" boasts the label on the DRiWATER® one-quart (liter) packages of gel-encased water. The gel is placed in an open-ended plastic tube that is buried in the soil near plant roots. Nature does the rest as the water is slowly released into the soil.

In July 1998 the scheduled first phase of the project was complete—a tract of desert containing a million blooming trees. The Egyptian government now offers subsidized water and land to families willing to leave the cities and move to the desert.

Here in the Sahara the future may spring from new and flourishing communities in a place where once only thirsty nomads roamed. Space-age technologies like DRiWATER® and reverse osmosis suggest that there is hope in facing future water problems.

Technology alone, however, is not the answer to the world's water problems. We all must become more aware of the river that flows through each of us, and each of us has a role to play in maintaining the water supply that sustains this river. ■

I often quote an African proverb that says: "The world is not ours, the earth is not ours. It's a treasure we hold in trust for future generations." And I often hope we will be worthy of that trust.

Kofi Annan

Interesting Facts . . .

- DRiWATER® wastes almost no water delivering it directly to plant roots.
- A 1 quart (1 liter) container of DRiWATER® lasts for about 3 months.
- When the DRiWATER® project in Egypt is complete, 17 million trees will provide materials, food, jobs, and a new atmosphere for the local desert community.
- DRiWATER® now also distributes its product in Israel, the United Kingdom, China, and Australia.
- Tunisia, the world's second-largest grower of olive trees, is proposing to establish a manufacturing facility somewhere in the country.

BIOGRAPHIES

ISABEL ALLENDE

Isabel Allende was born in Lima, Peru, in 1942. Her father was a Chilean diplomat and her godfather is Salvador Allende, the former President of Chile.

In her early twenties she worked for the Food and Agriculture Organization of the United Nations in a program called The Hunger Campaign. Her early writing work was in Chile, authoring articles for a radical women's magazine, and producing her own television program. In 1973 Salvador Allende was assassinated by Augusto Pinochet who then instituted a brutal repressive regime forcing her to flee to Venezuela.

In 1981 she began working on her first novel, *The House of the Spirits*, which was a great critical and financial success. From this success she published *Of Love and Shadows* in 1986, *Eva Luna* in 1991 and *Daughter of Fortune* in 1999. She wrote *Paula*, her autobiography, while telling the story of her life to her dying daughter Paula.

KOFI ANNAN

Kofi Annan was born in 1938 in Ghana. He holds a bachelors degree from Macalester College in Minnesota and a master's degree in management from MIT in 1972. Annan began his career in the UN organization in 1962 working in management for the World Health Organization, the High Commissioner for Human Rights, and the UN Economic Commission for Africa. From 1993 until 1995 he headed the United Nations Peacekeeping office, and in 1995 was responsible for about 70,000 peacekeepers in 77 countries. In 1997 he was elected to the post of Secretary-General of the United Nations.

While in office he has restored respect for the organization around the world by reducing waste and corruption and meeting world challenges head on. Facing a shortage of funds because of the refusal of the US Congress to pay back dues, he reached out to the corporate community to begin a dialogue on partnerships for sustainable development. In 1999 he proposed The Global Compact, nine principles on human rights, labor standards, and standards for the environment for corporations to adopt. He continues his role as an international statesman building bridges to a more peaceful world.

JAMES EARL CARTER

Jimmy Carter was born in Plains, Georgia, on October 1, 1924, and grew up on a peanut farm. In 1946 he graduated from the US Naval Academy in Annapolis, Maryland, and served seven years in the Navy. In 1962 he was elected Governor of Georgia where he served until 1976, when he was elected President of the United States of America. While President he fostered a national energy policy, created the Department of Education and brokered the historic Camp David peace treaty between Egypt and Israel.

After leaving the White House he opened the Carter Center in Georgia to promote peace and human rights and health issues around the world. The Center has projects in over 65 countries. President Carter has also been active in numerous countries monitoring the electoral process to ensure free and fair elections. Throughout his career he has kept in touch with his heritage, maintaining the family farm operation.

JOHAN CRUYFF

Johan Cruyff was born on April 25, 1947, in Betondorp, Holland. At the age of 10 he was drafted by the Dutch soccer team Ajax. While playing for the club as a teenager he convinced the team to hire his mother as a cleaner. Seven years after he started with the club he made the major league team. With Holland he won three consecutive European Cup championships and led the team to the World Cup finals. He won the title of European Footballer of the Year in 1971, 1973, and 1974. After his playing career he coached the Barcelona team to another European Cup win.

His influence over the game changed the face of European soccer. Since retiring from coaching he has helped countless children through the Johan Cruyff Welfare Foundation.

THE DALAI LAMA

His Holiness the 14th Dalai Lama Tenzin Gyatso, was born in 1935 to a peasant family. At the age of two he was recognized as the reincarnation of the 13th Dalai Lama. After the Chinese invasion of Tibet in 1949-1950 he tried for nine years to negotiate with Chinese officials to regain freedom for his people.

After years of frustration he was forced to flee to India in 1959, where he established a government in exile. Recognizing the danger of losing a whole culture, he established Tibetan arts and educational centers in India.

Since his exile he has lobbied tirelessly around the world on behalf of the people of Tibet. In all his efforts he has steadfastly refused any call to violence and for this he was awarded the Nobel Peace Prize in 1989. As both head of state and spiritual leader of the Tibetan people, he continues daily in his efforts to free Tibet from Chinese occupation, traveling and speaking all over the world.

TED DANSON

Ted Danson was born in 1947, and raised near a Navajo reservation in Arizona, the son of an archaeologist. He studied at both Stanford University and Carnegie Tech. His early acting work was in commercials and soap operas. He broke into movies in 1978 with a small part in *The Onion Field* and in 1981 was cast in the television role of Sam Malone, the barkeep of *Cheers*. Eleven years in this role propelled him to superstardom and he continues to work in both TV and movies.

In 1987 Danson founded the American Oceans Campaign to raise awareness of the dangers facing our national coastlines. Among AOC projects is a lobbying effort for the passage of the BEACH bill in the US Congress and a campaign to stop the practice of bottom trolling, which destroys vast areas of ocean bottom habitat each year. This group continues to be in the forefront of activism in the battle to stop the destruction of coastal environments.

MIKHAIL GORBACHEV

Born in 1931 in the city of Privolnoye, Mikhail Gorbachev spent many of his early years working on a collective farm. In 1952 he became a full member of the Communist Party. He holds degrees from Moscow State University Law School and Stavropol Agricultural Institute. With a new agricultural degree he was appointed Second Secretary Stavropol Kraikom, responsible for agriculture in 1968. His success in agricultural output from the Stavropol region propelled him up through party ranks, and in 1978 he received the Order of the October Revolution. Gorbachev was Head of Agriculture, and in 1985 he was elected General Secretary of the Central Committee in charge of the Soviet Union.

His new policy of *glasnost*, or openness, ultimately led to the fall of the Berlin Wall and the demise of the Soviet Union. In 1990 he was awarded the Nobel Peace Prize for his efforts. Currently he heads Green Cross International and travels the world promoting environmental issues.

QUEEN NOOR OF JORDAN

Born Lisa Najeeb Halaby in 1951, Queen Noor of Jordan grew up in Washington, D.C., the daughter of a former US Navy test pilot. Her father was head of the Federal Aviation Administration under President Kennedy. She holds a degree in architecture and urban planning from Princeton University. She put this degree to work on early jobs in Australia and in Teheran. In 1976 her father accepted the task of rebuilding the Jordanian Airlines, and she moved with him to Jordan taking the job of Director of Facilities Planning and Design for the project.

It was during this time that she met and was courted by King Hussein. They were married on June 15, 1978, and she took the name Noor al-Hussein, "Light of Hussein."

In her position as Queen she worked to preserve Jordan's cultural heritage and to advance the causes of Arab women and children. While not overtly political, she has not been afraid to criticize her native country when she felt it could do more to advance the cause of peace in the Middle East. Her husband developed cancer in 1992 and her strength and grace helped guide the nation of Jordan through the tragedy of King Hussein's death in 1999.

SHIMON PERES

Shimon Peres was born in Poland in 1923. In 1934 his family immigrated to Tel Aviv. He spent years working on a kibbutz and was elected Secretary of the Youth Labor Party in 1943. He was conscripted and worked on arms procurement and recruitment during Israel's war for independence in 1947. In 1952 he was appointed Deputy Director-General of the Ministry of Defense and was Director-General between 1953 and 1959. He has served as Minister of Immigrant Absorption, Minister of Transport and Communications, Minister of Information, and Minister of Foreign Affairs.

In 1984 he was elected Prime Minister of Israel. In 1989 he won the Nobel Peace Prize. He has written several books and recently established the Peres Center for Peace to work on issues of peace in the troubled Middle East. He is still a member of the Knesset and active in Israeli politics as well as a statesman on a variety of global issues.

ANITA RODDICK

Born in 1942, Anita Roddick grew up in Littlehampton, England. Her degree is from Newton Park College and, before opening The Body Shop, she held jobs teaching, working for a newspaper, and working for the United Nations. Through her extensive travels she gained an appreciation for how women around the world used simple, natural products to care for their bodies. In 1976, she opened a small cosmetic shop to support her two children while her husband was away in the Americas.

Using environmentally friendly ingredients and processes, she grew The Body Shop into a multi million-dollar business. She has used The Body Shop as a model and a platform for socially responsible development. She received London's Business Woman of the Year Award in 1985, and both the Order of the British Empire Award and the United Nations Global 500 Environmental Award in 1988. She continues to challenge businesses and the world financial community to find ways to meet the needs of a growing global population in a socially conscious, sustainable manner.

INTERNET SITES

■ CHAPTER ONE
TAMPERING WITH MOTHER NATURE

The Namib Desert—Disturbing the Balance
http://www.courtneymilne.com/namib/namib.html
http://www.fao.org/desertification/default.asp?lang=en
http://www.go2africa.com/namibia/namib-desert/namib-desert

Glen Canyon Dam—Altering the Flow
http://www.glencanyon.org/
http://water.usgs.gov/pubs/FS/FS-089-96/
http://www.usbr.gov/cdams/dams/glencanyon.html

The Biesbosch—A Wetland in Trouble
http://www.wetlands.agro.nl/
http://www.biesboschmuseum.nl/biesbosch.html
http://www.sierraclub.org/wetlands/

Guardians of the Rainforest
http://www.cofan.org/
http://www.ecuadorable.com/amazonia/cofan.htm
http://www.therainforestsite.com/cgi-bin/WebObjects/RainforestSite

■ CHAPTER TWO
THE SPIRIT OF WATER

Japanese Tea Ceremony—A Way of Life
http://www.urasenke.or.jp/eframe.html
http://www.tokujo.ac.jp/Tanaka/WWW97/Hello6/tomomi.html
http://www.art.uiuc.edu/japanhouse/tea/

Blessing of the Harvest in Bali—An Amazing Grace
http://www.bali-plus.com/harvest.htm
http://www.khandro.net/all_%20about_rice.htm
http://www.britannica.com/bcom/eb/article/9/0,5716,118219+10,00.html

Initiation of a Shinto Priest—Contact with the Gods
http://www.trincoll.edu/zines/tj/tj4.4.96/articles/cover.html
http://www.asahi-jc.com/shrine.html
http://www.geocities.com/Athens/8871/rituals.html

Baptism in the Jordan—Down by the Riverside
http://www.flc.org/central/israel/day3.htm
http://personal.nbnet.nb.ca/heaven11/sac/baptism/theology.htm
http://www.twosco.com/baptism_site.html

Cremation at Varanasi—The Most Holy Death
http://www.tapezismus.de/religionen/english/hinism8.html
http://ccwf.cc.utexas.edu/~hsc/hindu.html
http://www.cnn.com/EARTH/9805/17/ganges.pollution.ap/

■ CHAPTER THREE
THE ENDLESS SEARCH

The Kalahari Bushmen—A Hunt for Hidden Water
http://www.britannica.com/bcom/eb/article/5/0,5716,66945+1+65258,00.html
http://www.kalaharipeoples.org/kpfmain.htm
http://www.teacher.co.za/9909/book.html

Petra—A Study of Ancient Engineering
http://www.brown.edu/Departments/Anthropology/Petra/
http://www.globalearn.com/expeditions/eme/eme_invest/eme_enviro/ien
14_petra.html
http://student.rwu.edu/users/ah1826/ah1826/Petra/PPPETRA.html

Cattle Ranching in the Australian Outback—Lessons From the Aborigines
http://cyberfair.gsn.org/acreekps/abointro.htm
http://www.australia.com.nf/Aboriginal%20Art/jinta5.htm
http://enso.unl.edu/ndmc/mitigate/policy/austral.htm

Nets in the Mist—The Fog Catchers of Chungungo
http://www.idrc.ca/nayudamma/fogcatc_72e.html
http://205.67.213.10/Fog/fog.htm
http://drylands.nasm.edu:1995/camanchaca.html

Mexico City—A Sinking Metropolis
http://lanic.utexas.edu/la/Mexico/water/book.html
http://gmac.uncc.edu/faculty/haas/geol3190/termpap/sommer/history.html
http://northcoast.com/~spdtom/a-links.html

■ CHAPTER FOUR
OUR DAILY WATER

Valencia, Spain—Learning to Live with Drought
http://ens.lycos.com/ens/sep99/1999L-09-24-05.html
http://www.pub.gov.sg/g2tip.html
http://www.ecodes.org/webagua2000/ingles.htm

Windhoek, Namibia—No Water to Waste
http://www.republikein.com.na/archive/Junie%202000/mark/woen2106/storie1.htm
http://www.irn.org/programs/okavango/wn.demand.shtml
http://www.uweb.ucsb.edu/~mtarr/how.html

Phoenix, Arizona—An Artificial Aura of Abundance
http://aggiehorticulture.tamu.edu/extension/xeriscape/xeriscape.html

■ CHAPTER FIVE
A PRICE TO PAY

The Water Bearers of Ajmer—Free Water at a Price
http://www.india-today.com/itoday/20000508/cover3.html
http://www.unv.org/projects/sl/collect/swrc2.htm

Britain's Private Water Companies—The Great Experiment
http://www.worldbank.org/html/fpd/notes/115/115summary.html
http://www.unesco.org/courier/1999_02/uk/dossier/txt21.htm
http://www.cupe.ca/arp/00/2.asp

Mirzapur, India—Rebuilding a Government System
http://users.boone.net/gibbons/
http://www.gisdevelopment.net/application/plandev/scott.htm
http://www.epw.org.in/34-52/disc.htm

Santiago, Chile—A Golden Business Opportunity
http://www.iclei.org/iclei/santiago.htm
http://www.wsp.org/English/wps-linkcvr.html
http://www.psiru.org/country/France/news.htm

■ CHAPTER SIX
THE AORTA OF AGRICULTURE

Rice—Feeding the World with Water
http://www.isnar.org/irri/
http://www.askasia.org/frclasrm/lessplan/l000008.htm
http://www.bali-plus.com/harvest.htm

Beef—It's Water for Dinner
http://hill.beef.org/stats/
http://www.iitap.iastate.edu/gcp/issues/society/ogallala/ogallala.html
http://www.EarthSave.org/

Drip Irrigation in Kenya—Low-Tech, Small Farms
http://www.ssu.missouri.edu/iap/Harambee/09_Irrigate.html
http://www.landfood.unimelb.edu.au/dean/falveybk/ch2.html
http://echonet.org/azillus/azch7dry.htm

Dutch Tomatoes—High-Tech, Big Business
http://ag.arizona.edu/hydroponictomatoes/
http://www.minlnv.nl/international/policy/plant/glas/infoippglas.htm
http://pages.prodigy.com/gardenshop/gdnshop3.htm

Aguas Negras—Irrigation in Mexico
http://www.iwrn.net/naranjo.htm
http://www.fao.org/docrep/T0551E/t0551e04.htm#2.2%20human%20exposure%20control
http://www.greywater.com/

■ CHAPTER SEVEN
THE WAY OF THE RIVER

The Nile—Blessing and Curse of Egypt
http://www.nilebasin.org/IntroNR.htm
http://www.nzz.ch/online/04_english/background/background2000/background0007/bg000722egypt.htm
http://remc12.k12.mi.us/kalamazoo-academy/mdonald.htm

The Aral Sea—Draining the Blood of a Nation
http://www.ifas-almaty.kz/
http://www.dfd.dlr.de/app/land/aralsee/
http://www.mhhe.com/biosci/pae/environmentalscience_map/aralsea.html

Three Gorges Dam—Taming the Dragon
http://www.coxnews.com/washington/GORGES.HTM
http://www.irn.org
http://www.usembassy-china.org.cn/english/sandt/3gorcab.htm

■ CHAPTER EIGHT
THE PIPELINE OF INDUSTRY

Steel—Using Water as a Cooling Agent
http://www.intercom.es/espadas/history.htm
http://www.worldsteel.org/
http://www.nsc.co.jp/english/ns_news/269/b.html#02

Paper—Using Water as a Processing Medium
http://www.usaep.org/reports/pulp.htm
http://www.wbcsd.ch/publications/paper1.htm
http://www.millarwestern.com/environment/index.html

Beer—Using Water as a Part of the Product
http://www.beerhistory.com/library/holdings/raley_timetable.shtml
http://www.heineken.com/no_flash_homepage.cfm
http://www.breworld.com/the_brewer/9610/water.html

■ CHAPTER NINE
THE PERILS OF POLLUTION

London, 1854—A Neighborhood of Plague
http://www.metrokc.gov/health/prevcont/cholera.htm
http://www.ph.ucla.edu/epi/snow.html
http://coursesa.matrix.msu.edu/~hst425/MCC1.htm

Diarrhea—An International Plague
http://www.thp.org/bangladesh/bangla998/
http://www.niddk.nih.gov/health/digest/pubs/diarrhea/diarrhea.htm#whatis
http://www.childreach.org/map/CIS/bangladesh.html

Moldova and Ukraine—A Lethal Legacy
http://bisnis.doc.gov/bisnis/isa/9711up.htm
http://www-esd.worldbank.org/ecssd/envcopg/esmold.html

Father Rhine—The Rebirth of a River
http://www.iksr.org/icpr/1uk.htm
http://www.unesco.org/courier/2000_06/uk/planet.htm
http://www.americanoceans.org/

■ CHAPTER TEN
THE CHALLENGE OF TRANSPORTATION

The Masai—A Walk of Life
http://www.denison.edu/enviro/envs245/papers/Massai/Maasai2.html
http://bvsd.k12.co.us/schools/cent/Newspaper/mar97/Masai.html
http://www.vaccines.ch/peh/ehn/ehn25.htm

The Aqueducts of Ancient Rome—A Grand System
http://www.lucknow.com/horus/etexts/frontinus.html
http://myron.sjsu.edu/romeweb/ENGINEER/art5a.htm
http://www.edmonds.wednet.edu/cyberschool/Students/Stocker/aqueducts_nathan.htm

The Central Arizona Project—Growing Cities in the Desert
http://www.cap-az.com/
http://www.water.az.gov/AZWaterInfo/coloradoriver/Default.htm
http://amrivers.localweb.com/10-most97.html

A Tale of Two Farmers—Spain's Tajo-Segura Project
http://www.hyd.uu.se/swm/watemanage.htm
http://www.sardi.sa.gov.au/hort/cit_page/gro_spca.htm
http://ens.lycos.com/ens/sep99/1999L-09-24-05.html

Water Bags—From Turkey to Cypress
http://www.waterbag.com/media/SFnews.htm
http://www.hri.org/news/cyprus/cmnews/97-10-09.cmnews.html
http://www.abcnews.go.com/sections/world/DailyNews/cypruswater980731.html

■ CHAPTER ELEVEN
WATER—WAR AND PEACE

Water Court of Valencia—Justice for Farmers, Decided by Farmers
http://www.comunidad-valenciana.com/english/urbano/valencia/pag1_1.htm
http://home.att.net/~intlh2olaw/useful_sites.htm
http://www.goodfruit.com/archive/Feb15-97/special5.html

Great Anatolia Project—A Turkish Dilemma
http://www.tusiad.org.tr/yayin/private/autumn98/html/sec12.html
http://www.library.utoronto.ca/pcs/thresh/thresh3.htm
http://www.washington-report.org/backissues/0390/9003055.htm

Draining Paradise—The Okavango River Dispute
http://www.mindspring.com/~johnbock/
http://www.stud.ntnu.no/~skjetnep/owls_2000.html
http://www.uweb.ucsb.edu/~mtarr/how.html

On the Edge of Crisis - The Arab-Israeli Conflict
http://www.ariga.com/treaties/annex2.html
http://www.israeleconomy.org/strategic/water.htm
http://www.ipsjps.org/html/water3.htm

■ CHAPTER TWELVE
FACING THE FUTURE

Sana'a—Running on Empty
http://www.worldbank.org/pics/pid/ye57602.txt
http://www.yemeninfo.gov.ye/ENGLISH/ECONOMY/moving.htm
http://www.mit.edu/afs/athena.mit.edu/org/a/akpia/www/AKPsite/4.239/sanaa/yemen.html

Los Angeles—Illusion of Abundance
http://www.monolake.org/socalwater/wctips.htm
http://www.ladwp.com/home.htm
http://www.monolake.org/

NASA—Water Out of This World
http://spacelink.nasa.gov/Instructional.Materials/NASA.Educational.Products/International.Space.Station.Clean.Water/
http://advlifesupport.jsc.nasa.gov/
http://www.tpwd.state.tx.us/expltx/eft/nasa/edeen/edeen1.htm

Desalination—Taking the Salt out of the Sea
http://urila.tripod.com//desalination.htm
http://www.environment.about.com/newsissues/environment/msubwat3.htm
http://dailypress.com/special/reservoir/resdesal4.htm

DRiWATER®—Planting a Forest in the Desert
http://www.driwater.com/

FILM CREDITS

Water: The Drop of Life is a companion to the Public Television Series "Water: The Drop of Life," which is a Swynk production in coproduction with NCRV, NOB, TVE S.A., and CPTV Connecticut.

This book is only possible because of the hard work of the following people on the production of the series:

Executive Producers
John Wegink
Peter Gersen

Series Director
Peter Swanson

Series Producer
Joost van Loon

Writers
Bob Field
Katherine Deutch Tatlock

Location Producers And Directors
Alexandra Jansse
Paul King

Interviews
Marion Versluys

Production Managers
Joseph Melskens
Elles Visser

Assistant Production Manager
Ingrid Sterrenburg

Narrator
Allan Zipson

Graphic Design
Jaap Drupsteen
Floris Drupsteen

Music
Jaap Eggermont
Peter Schön
Bernhard Joosten
Frank Burks

Editors
Sándor Soeteman
Saskia Buren
Dolf Fresen

Research
Margreet Plukker
Myra Konings
Karen Hoy
Linda de Veer
Ariane Greep
Margaret Massop
Nicole van Damme
Brenda de Jager
Arthur van Amerongen
Pam Parker

Photography
Peter Lataster
Anton van Munster (N.S.C.)
Gilles Frenken
Erik Bannenberg
Daniël Gallenkamp
Jan van den Nieuwenhuijzen
Jan van Lennep
Paul Cohen
Arnoud Gravestein
Bob Noll

Camera Assistance
Martin Struijf
Pieter Huisman
Louise Oeben
Dennis Wielaert
Stefano Bertacchini
Stefan Bijnen
Laureline Smith
Nina da Costa
Mike Peterson

Sound Recording
Rinie Jansen
Peter Westbroek
Upe van Leeuwen
John Davelaar
Martijn van Haalen
Andries Stoker
Axel Haringa
Wouter Hasebos
Lincoln Morrison
Bruce Spero

Technical Facilities
Nob Fieldproduction
Nob Postproduction
Cineco Film Laboratorium

Production Assistants
Charlotte Immink
Eelke Bokelman

Production Accountants
Astrid Goudsbloem
Marcel van der Avort

Postproduction
André De Laat
Peter Rump
Ingeborg de Buijzer
Gert Jan de Vries
Glenn Thomas
Gert Jan Eijlers
Mark Dubbeldam
Hans van Eijken
Ronald van Dieren
Martin Klein

Consultants
Willem van Kooten
Allerd Stikker
Henk Donkers
Mark Verkerk

Co-Producers NCRV/Euro Ficción S.L.
Pieter Schut
Carlos Orengo
Stefan Nicoll

Station Relations
Signe Hovde

National Corporate Sponsorships
Donna Collins
Scott Phillips

PBS Business Relations
Dana O'Neil

Promotional Partner
Civilization Magazine

Outreach Partner
Water Environment Federation

The film series was made possible with the support of:
Heineken
ITT Industries
Young & Rubican Group
KPN-Station 12
Novib
Norit
Ministry of Foreign Affairs–Development Cooperation
Directorate General of Public Works and Water Management
Developed with support of The MEDIA program of the European Union

INDEX

Aborgines, 40-41
Africa, 36, 73, 106, 122
Aguas negras, 75
Ajmer, India, 58-59
Allende, Isabel, 11, 27, 30, 34, 37, 40, 42, 43, 51, 56, 64, 104, 106, 110, 126, 132
Amazon River, 22
Annan, Kofi, 8, 13, 26, 33, 65, 66, 69, 73, 76, 82, 116, 122, 137
Aqueducts, 108-109
Aral Sea, 80-82
Aswan Dam, 78
Australia, 40

Bali, 27
Bangladesh, 98-99
Baptism, 30
Beef, 40, 70-72
Beer, 92-93
Biesbosch, 20-21

Canada, 91
Carter, Jimmy, 12, 66, 68, 71, 81, 96, 101, 118, 128
Central Arizona Project, 53-55, 110-112
China, 83
Chungungo, Chile,42-43
Cofan, 22-23
Colorado River, 18, 19
Cremation, 32-33
Cruyff, Johan, 9, 20, 46, 48, 50, 136
Cypress, 113

Dalai Lama, The, 9, 14, 16, 23, 46, 49, 115, 129
Danson, Ted, 9, 13, 17, 19, 24, 46, 52, 54, 76, 86, 89, 92, 97, 109, 112, 126, 130, 135
Desalination, 134-135
Drip irrigation, 73, 74
DRiWATER®, 136-137

Ecuador, 22-23
Egypt, 78, 90, 125
Euphrates River, 120-121

Fog Catchers, 42-43

Ganges River, 32, 62
GAP project, 120-121
Glenn Canyon Dam, 18-19
Gorbachev, Mikhail, 11, 76, 80, 85, 86, 94, 103, 104, 133, 137
Great Britain, 60-61, 62

Iraq, 120
Israel, 74, 124

Japan, 26, 28, 68, 88-89
Japanese Tea Ceremony, 26
Jordan River, 30-31, 124

Kalahari Desert, 36-37, 122
Kenya, East Africa, 73

London, England, 96-97
Los Angeles, California, 54, 130-131

Masai, 9, 106, 107
Mexico, 44-45, 54, 75
Mirzapur, India, 62-63
Mist nets, 42-43
Moldova, 100-101
Mono Lake, 130-131

Namibia, 16-17, 50, 122-123
NASA, 132-133
Netherlands, 20, 74, 102, 126
Nile River, 78-79, 90

Ogallala Aquifer, 70-71
Okavango River, 122-123

Paper, 90-91
Peres, Shimon, 8, 14, 21, 22, 34, 36, 41, 59, 63, 66, 72, 74, 79, 110, 111, 116, 134
Petra, Jordan, 38-39
Phoenix, Arizona, 53, 110-113
Privatization, 60-61

Queen Noor of Jordan, 12, 24, 31, 34, 39, 44, 121, 123

Rainforest, 22-23
Rhine River, 20, 102-103
Rice, 68-69
Rift Valley, 73, 79, 106-107
Roddick, Anita, 12, 14, 28, 29, 56, 86, 93, 107

Sahara Desert, 50, 136
Sana'a, 128-129
Santiago, Chile, 64-65
Shinto Priests, 28-29
Spain, 48, 88, 114-115, 118-119
Steel, 88-89
Syria, 120-121, 125

Tajo–Segura Project, 114-115
Thailand, 92
Three Gorges Dam, 83-85
Transportation, 104-115
Turkey, 113, 120-121

Ukraine, 100-101
United States, 53, 70, 110-113, 130-131, 132-133

Valencia, Spain, 48-49, 50, 118-119
Varanasi, India, 32-33

Wastewater, 75
Wetlands, 20, 21
Windhoek, Namibia, 50-52

Xeriscape®, 55

Yangtze River, 83
Yarmuk River, 124
Yemen, 128-129